Revolution IN THE LYMES

Revolution in the Lymes

From the New Lights to the Sons of Liberty

Jim Lampos and Michaelle Pearson

The History Press

Published by The History Press
Charleston, SC
www.historypress.net

First published 2016

Manufactured in the United States

ISBN 978.1.46713.596.2

Library of Congress Control Number: 2016945797

To our children, Phoebe and Silvanos, with love.

Contents

Acknowledgements

The authors wish to thank the following for their assistance:

The Connecticut Historical Society
The Connecticut State Library
The East Lyme Historical Society
The Florence Griswold Museum and Lyme Historical Society
The Fraunces Tavern Museum
The Lyme Local History Archives/Lyme Public Hall Association
The Massachusetts Historical Society
The New London County Historical Society
The New York Public Library
The Old Lyme Historical Society
The Old Lyme–Phoebe Griffin Noyes Library

With special thanks to:

Linda Alexander, Carolyn Bacdayan, Ann Brubaker, Kayla Correll, Robert Couteau, Mary Fiorelli, Elizabeth Kuchta, Jessica Phillips and Nicole Wholean.

Chapter 1
INTRODUCTION

Thunder came down the Post Road from Meetinghouse Hill, just past midnight. The roar grew louder, more insistent, and the ground shook. Reverend Stephen Johnson was awakened by the sound. Listening closely, he realized what it was: hoofbeats. A rider galloping swiftly down the hill, throwing clods up from the road recently cleared of snows from the winter gales.

He arose and dressed quickly, his heart pounding through his body; but the more insistent pounding came from without, not within. Had the thunders of Divine Providence arrived at his door, stood at attention and knocked? Could those thunders be summoned as the alchemists of old had promised, as the learned Governor John Winthrop had intimated? Yes. The thunder was at his door, and he flew down the stairs to answer. Who would impose upon his home at this ungodly hour, pounding with the force of a storm, on this day, April 21, in the year of our Lord 1775, and for what reason? Johnson threw open his threshold and beheld a man he knew well. Israel Bissel, having frantically ridden without rest from Worcester, spoke his urgent message: "TO ARMS! TO ARMS! THE WAR HAS BEGUN!" Johnson was alarmed but not surprised. He'd been waiting and preparing, for he knew this moment would come. Indeed, his pen was the cause of it.

Before a single shot is fired in battle, a more profound war of ideas has already been fought and decided, well in advance of a single soldier

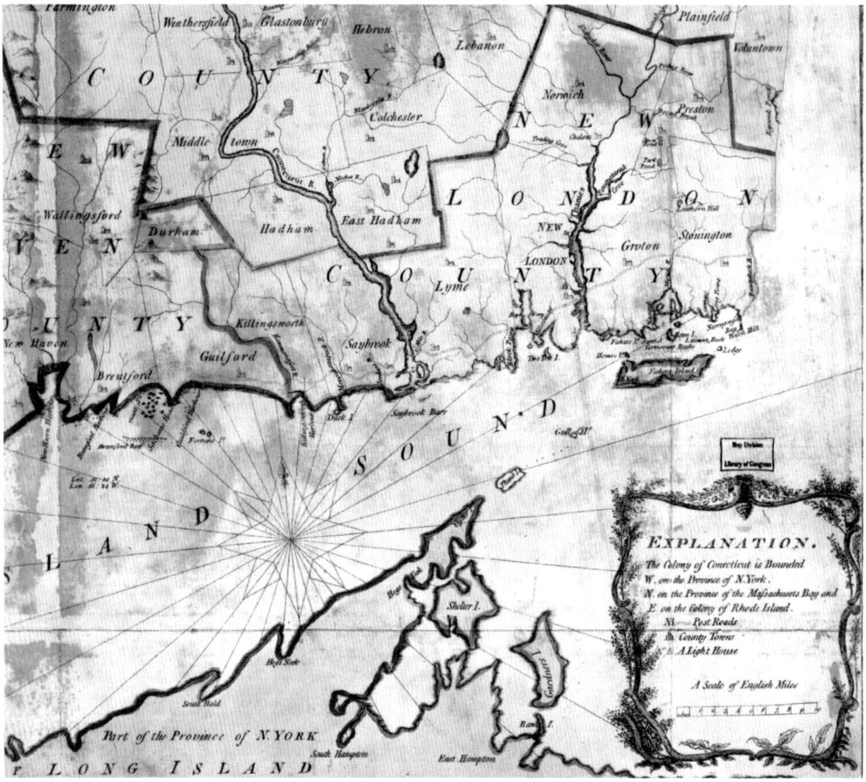

Moses Park map, 1766. *University of Connecticut Map Collection.*

being sent out to shed his blood in proof. Reverend Stephen Johnson's seditious writing against Britain's Stamp Act in 1765 had already secured his legacy as a Patriot and set the colonies on the path to revolution. Within hours of receiving the alarm, Johnson organized Lyme's militia to answer the call at Lexington. By summer, the reverend would be marching to Bunker Hill.

The striking aspect of Lyme's role in the American Revolution is the dedication of its leading citizens to the patriotic cause. Matthew Griswold, the most prominent member of Lyme's founding family; Reverend Stephen Johnson, the minister of the Congregational church; John McCurdy, the wealthiest merchant in the colony; and Samuel Holden Parsons, a leading attorney and professional soldier, all immediately and zealously took up the cause of liberty. For a town of such long-standing traditions, stability and wealth, the lack of British sympathies is as remarkable as the unambiguous patriotic dedication of its leaders.

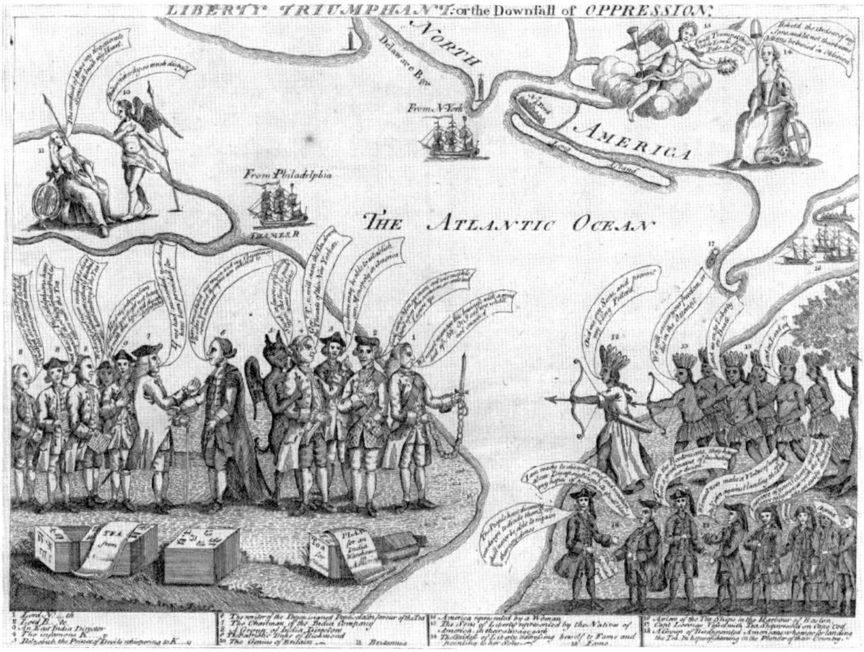

Liberty Triumphant, or the Downfall of Oppression, 1785, likely London. *New York Public Library.*

The origins of the American rebellion can be traced to the 1740s and even further, to the founding of the colonies during the English Civil War. The founders of Lyme were not humble pilgrims, but Cromwellians, part of the movement fighting King Charles I. With Cromwell's victory, Lyme enjoyed a great deal of independence and self-governance.

The confluence of scientific discoveries, world exploration, trade and philosophical inquiry based on a revival of classical principles sparked a new paradigm of thought that would inspire intellectuals, ministers, merchants and entrepreneurs from the mid-seventeenth century through the eighteenth. It was a world that was becoming at once more potent and magical while its myths were being dispelled and its rulers depotentiated. Alchemists embraced the occult while also experimenting with scientific principles that would rationalize their world. They sought both the purification of the spirit and the creation of wealth and tried to develop tools that would give them both at will. In doing so, they walked an invisible line between the enchanted and material worlds. Governor and alchemist John Winthrop the Younger single-handedly halted Connecticut's persecution of witchcraft. By the 1730s, New England's Christian ministers, such as Lyme's Reverend

Jonathan Parsons, acknowledged in their sermons that thunderstorms were not messages from God but natural occurrences that could be understood through scientific inquiry. By the time of the Revolution, the nation's leading intellectual divine, Ezra Stiles, was berating preachers and others who saw earthquakes and other natural disasters as evidence of God's judgment. This process of embracing scientific inquiry in their pursuit of spiritual grace had another result that naturally followed suit: it was no longer possible to justify the authority of kings on the basis of "divine right." In politics as well as religion, a more refined understanding of the world was taking shape.

Let us begin then in 1635. The dramatis personae include John Winthrop and the Cromwellians who hired him to establish the colony of Saybrook, of which Lyme was then a part, before the Saybrook Colony lost its autonomy and became part of Connecticut Colony.

Chapter 2

The Cromwellians of Saybrook Colony

Bind your king with chains and your nobles with fetters of iron, preached the Reverend Hugh Peters, one of the founders of Saybrook Colony. Peters, a Cambridge-educated radical Puritan cleric, left England and migrated first to Holland, then to Saybrook, in July 1635 to avoid the religious inquisition of King Charles I's Star Chamber Court.

Reverend Peters officially joined the Parliamentary forces of the English Civil War in 1641, when he was invited by the Earl of Warwick, Sir Thomas Fairfax, and Oliver Cromwell to meet in the English town of Lyme to plan their strategy for challenging the king.

The founding of Saybrook Colony came at a pivotal moment in history—the dawn of the Enlightenment—an age of exploration, new technology and ideas. It was an era that produced the Royal Society in England, which counted Sir Isaac Newton and Saybrook's Governor John Winthrop Jr. as members. The society was dedicated to empirical research and the dissemination of scientific ideas, as the art of alchemy was evolving into the discipline of chemistry. New ideas, technologies and innovations caused an economic boom in Western Europe, and a new class of independently wealthy entrepreneurs and investors began rising to power.

In England, the constitution guaranteed a balance of three estates: the king, the House of Lords and the House of Commons. No tax could be levied or law enacted without the consent of these three equally sovereign bodies. But new economies and philosophies meant a shift in the balance

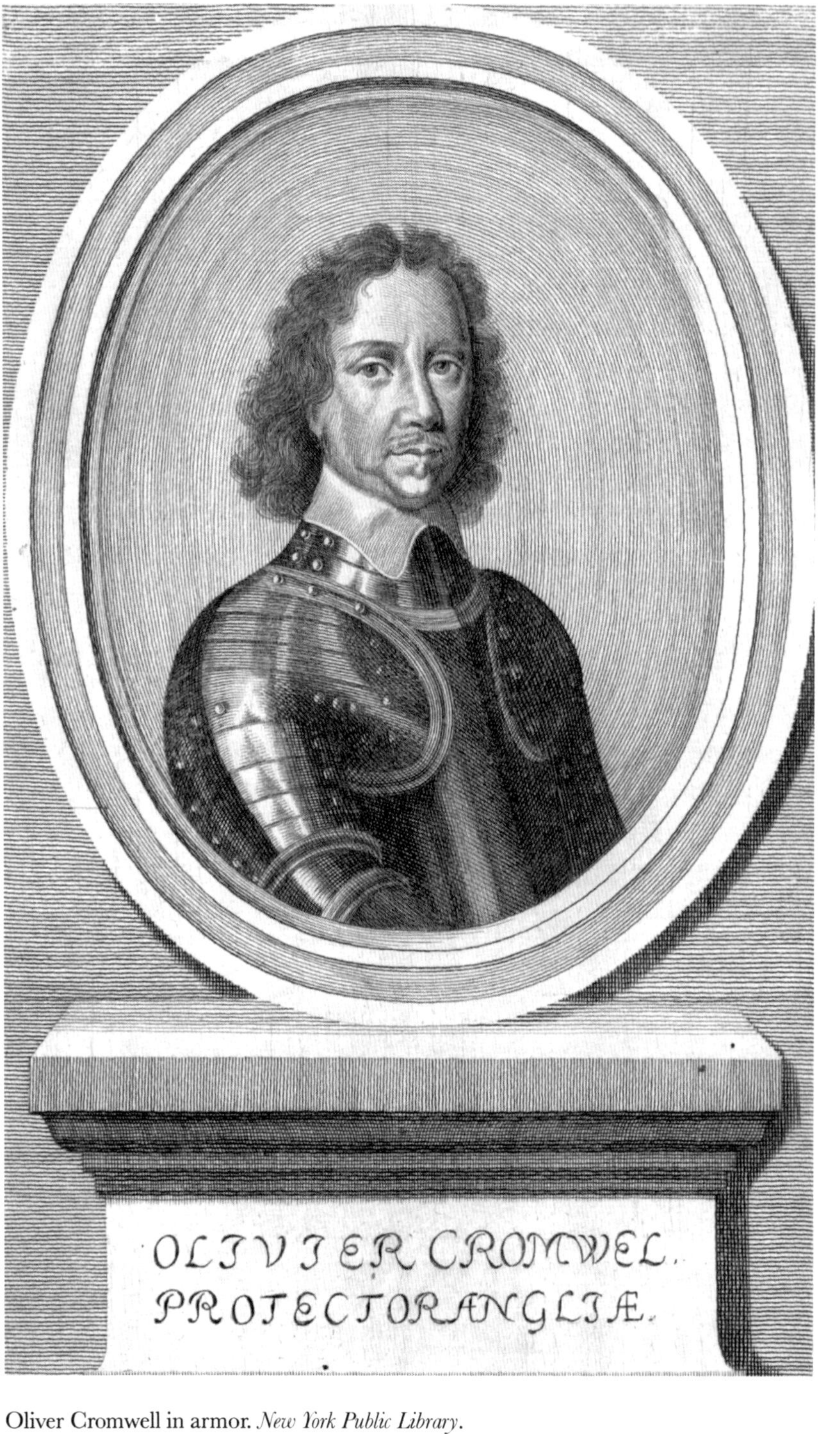

Oliver Cromwell in armor. *New York Public Library*.

of power, and when the House of Commons opposed King Charles's tax on shipping, England began to slip toward civil war.

The more King Charles sought to exert his authority, the more Parliament pushed back. The final straw came when Charles, on dubious counsel from his ministers, sent armed forces into the House of Commons to arrest the opposition. Parliament responded by raising its own Parliamentary army, and with Oliver Cromwell at its helm and Reverend Hugh Peters as chaplain, the war was engaged. It was a war that Charles I would lose, along with his head, on January 30, 1649.

Saybrook was founded as a place to "receive men of qualitie": the supporters of Cromwell. The colony was to be a refuge should they need to flee England and set up a government in exile. The Colony of Saybrook was established under a patent issued by Robert Rich, Earl of Warwick: the same man who had met with Hugh Peters and Cromwell in Lyme, England. Rich would subsequently become an influential member of Cromwell's forces. On March 19, 1631, he issued what came to be known as the Warwick Patent, conveying Saybrook as an independent colony to eleven patentees, primarily relatives, such as Sir Nathaniel Rich; and close associates, including William Fiennes, Viscount Saye and Sele; and Robert Greville, Lord Brooke. These men were involved in multiple enterprises in the Americas. For governor of Saybrook Colony, the patentees chose John Winthrop the Younger. Alchemist, occultist, physician, astronomer, pioneer and venture capitalist, Winthrop was a man well known to them by virtue of his talents and connections. In July 1635, Winthrop married Elizabeth Reade, Hugh Peters's stepdaughter. The next day, he accepted a one-year commission as governor of Saybrook Colony.

The Connecticut River was under Dutch authority at the time, but they had merely set up trading posts with light fortifications and no permanent settlements. The English saw an opportunity. Knowing the Dutch were primarily concerned with holding New Amsterdam and unwilling to seriously defend Saybrook and Hartford, the English seized Connecticut. In November 1635, John Winthrop dispatched an advance party to run off the Dutch and take control of Saybrook Point. After taking possession, Winthrop was charged with hiring three hundred men: a fifty-man crew to till Saybrook's soil, a fifty-man team of carpenters to construct homes fit for "men of qualitie" and a two-hundred-man garrison to defend the newest English colony, Fort Saybrook. Up to 1,500 acres would be reserved for nobles, including a large tract for Oliver Cromwell—the planned site of a great mansion to serve as his home when he arrived.

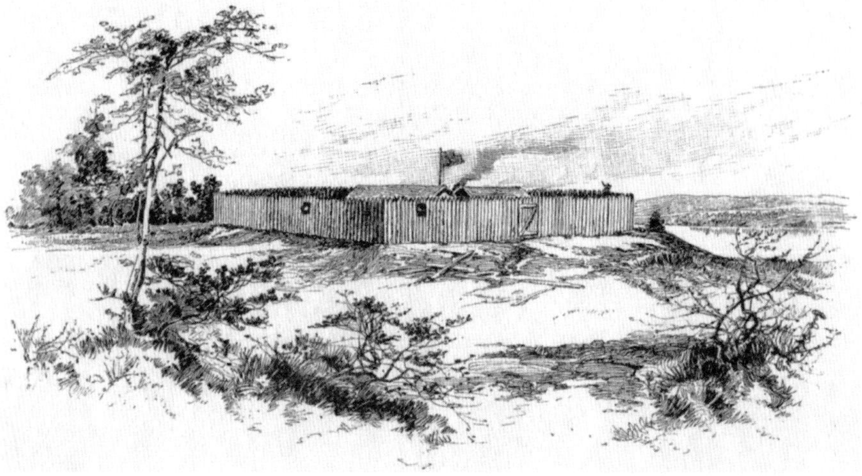

Saybrook Fort in 1636. Wood engraving. *New York Public Library*.

While living in Boston, where his father, John Winthrop the Elder, was governor, Winthrop had made the acquaintance of Lieutenant Lion Gardiner, a man hired by the elder Winthrop to construct a fortress at Fort Hill. In testament to his skills, the fortress Gardiner built was still in use 140 years later—the British garrisoned troops there during the Battle of Bunker Hill and the siege of Boston.

Prior to his arrival in Boston, Gardiner's ability as a military engineer had been well established in Holland. England and Holland had a military alliance at the time, so travel and commerce between the two nations were relatively fluid. In Holland, Gardiner met the exiled Reverend Peters and the dissenting London divine and future founder of New Haven, Reverend John Davenport. Winthrop the Younger knew that Gardiner was the man he needed to make Saybrook a success. Peters and Davenport convinced Gardiner to accept his most challenging commission: the construction of a fortress and settlement in the new colony of Saybrook at the mouth of the Connecticut River.

By March 1636, Gardiner arrived with twenty men and was actively working on the fortifications and settlement. Governor Winthrop landed one month later, accompanied by his father-in-law, Hugh Peters, and the only actual patentee under the Warwick Patent to settle at Saybrook, Colonel George Fenwick.

Fenwick was a lawyer and a soldier and, through the agency of his wife, Lady Alice, daughter of Sir Edward and Lady Apsley of Sussex, became a committed

Reverend Hugh Peters. *New York Public Library.*

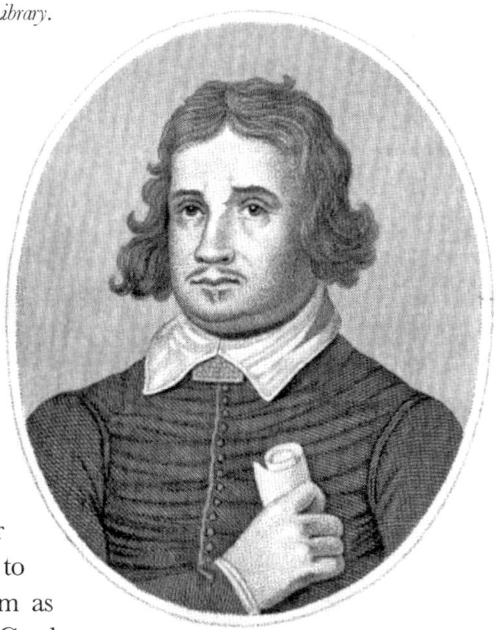

supporter of the Puritan and Parliamentarian cause. Meeting the Reverends Peters and Davenport in Holland, Fenwick helped procure supplies to be shipped to Saybrook Colony.

In 1635, Fenwick arrived with Peters in Boston, and the next spring he embarked with Winthrop and Peters for Saybrook. Winthrop returned to England in 1636 when his term as governor expired, and Lion Gardner took his place as Saybrook's chief magistrate. Fenwick took over in 1639, when, after the expiration of his term, Gardiner took possession of the Isle of Wight, later renamed Gardiner's Island, just across the Long Island Sound from Saybrook.

Fenwick's term as Saybrook's governor was difficult, but the colony slowly prospered and set the solid groundwork for its future success. Under his leadership, the New England Confederation of Colonies was formed in Boston in 1643. The confederation helped the colonies cooperate on issues of mutual interest and gave them an identity apart from their mother country. Saybrook did not have identity issues. The founders knew who they were and what they were about. They were loyal subjects of the king so long as their king was loyal to them, not only as fellow Englishmen, but as free people endowed with the right to determine their own affairs.

Saybrook was unlike the other colonies of America. It was independent long before 1776. The colonies of New Hampshire, New York, the Carolinas and Georgia were under direct royal control, meaning they had to clear their legislation with London and were bound by royal orders. Massachusetts, Maryland and Pennsylvania were under partial control. But Saybrook was founded as an independent corporate entity, empowered to decide its own affairs. In this respect, it was closest to the autonomous colonies of Connecticut, New Haven and Rhode Island.

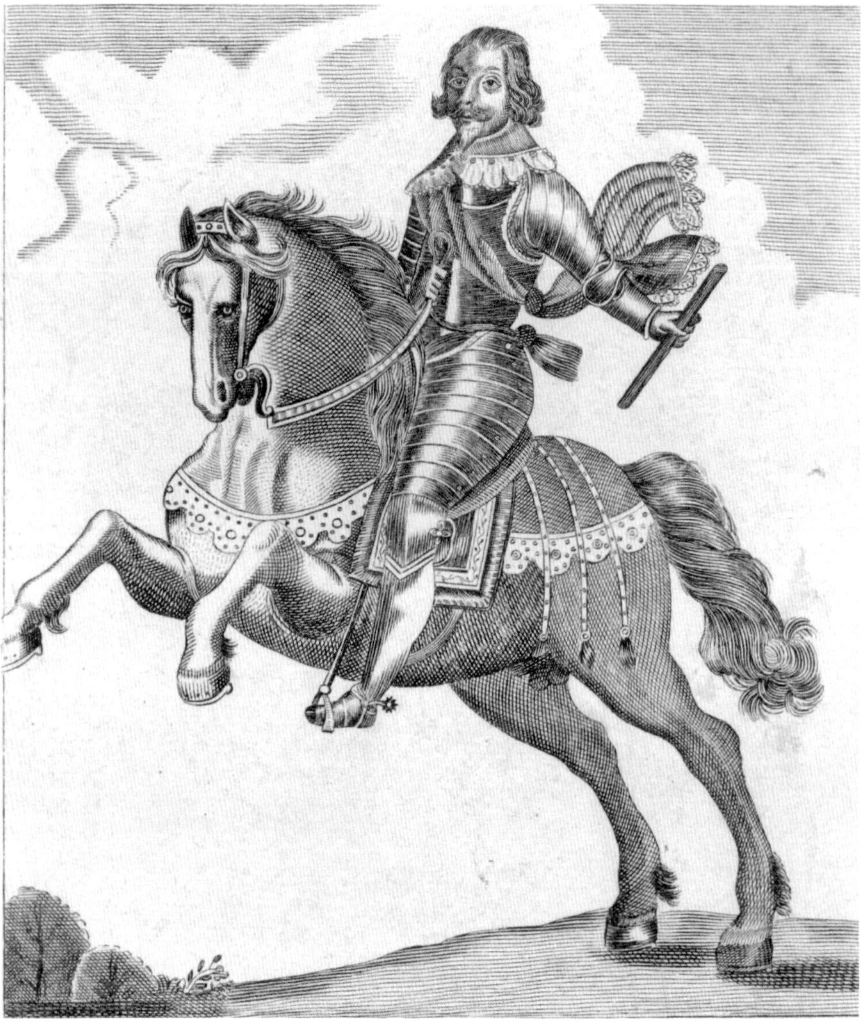

Viscount Saye and Sele. *New York Public Library.*

Saybrook's right to self-determination did not end when Fenwick sold it to the Colony of Connecticut in 1645 for approximately $900,000 in today's money. It is important to note that Fenwick did not sell the land but merely the fort at Saybrook and political control over the region. Although it was now a town rather than an independent colony, Saybrook retained the power to determine its own affairs locally through town meetings of freemen, and on the colonial level it kept the power to elect its representatives to the General Assembly of Connecticut. This was an extraordinary measure of independence and a rather unique state of affairs in the political world of colonial America at the time.

The success of the Parliamentarians' cause and Cromwell's military assault on the king's men proved to be Saybrook's undoing. As Cromwell consolidated power throughout the 1640s, it became clear that not only would the Parliamentarians not need to flee to Saybrook, but they might also soon rule England.

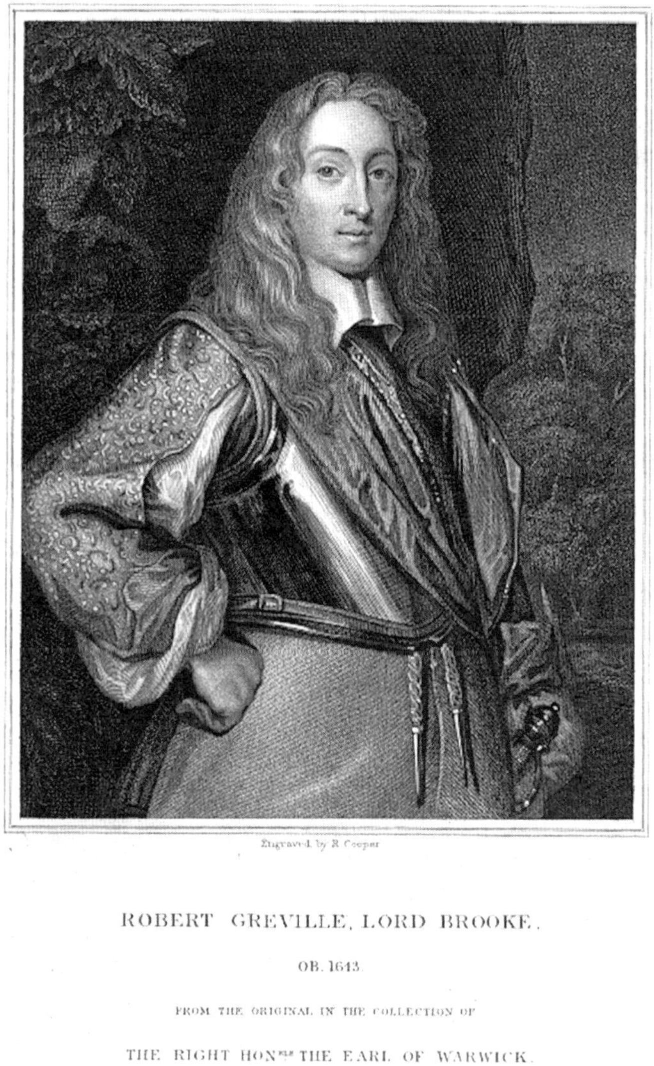

Lord Brooke. *New York Public Library*.

Hugh Peters returned to England in 1641 to join Cromwell, and Fenwick left in 1645 after the death of his wife and the end of his commission. Upon returning to England, Fenwick commanded regiments under Cromwell, took part in the invasion of Scotland, was appointed to the trial of King Charles I, became a member of Parliament under the Protectorate and finally served as governor of Edinburgh Castle.

Saybrook languished in this period, as its reason for being—a seat for the Cromwellian government in exile—ceased to be with the victory of the Parliamentarians and the execution of the king.

However, this period proved critical to its development. Saybrook was now left to its own devices, with little supervision from England's Lord Protector Oliver Cromwell. Thus, the period between 1645 and 1660 lay the groundwork for a political realm committed to self-reliance and self-determination by a populace with the fortitude and will to defend itself against all who would trespass against that sovereignty, including the English monarch, after Charles II took the throne in the Restoration following Cromwell's death.

The heroes of the Parliamentary movement in the English Civil War met ignoble fates with the Restoration. Hugh Peters was arrested by Charles II and beheaded at Charing Cross on October 16, 1660. Those who had already died, including Cromwell, were exhumed, their corpses beheaded and remains defiled and whatever was left reinterred in unsanctified, and often unmarked, graves. Remarkably, a few stalwart characters, like John Winthrop the Younger, not only survived both the Cromwellian period and Restoration but also flourished.

The lines separating the two sides of the English Civil War were often hazy and ill defined. Nobles, clergy and military men of the same class were often on opposite sides and sometimes even switched sides. William Fiennes, the Viscount Saye and Sele, for example, though a supporter of Cromwell at the outset, was glad to see Charles II take the throne and restore the monarchy to Britain. The most unique character, though, was Winthrop. Though closely associated with Cromwell, he managed, as governor of Connecticut, to secure a charter from Charles II that gave not only official authorization and recognition to the Connecticut colony but also as nearly a degree of complete political autonomy as one could ever imagine in colonial America.

The agency through which Winthrop was able to reach Charles II, and convince him to grant this liberal charter, was a somewhat shadowy and mysterious organization, a fraternity that calls itself a "craft" and first came into public view through official bodies and a recorded meeting in

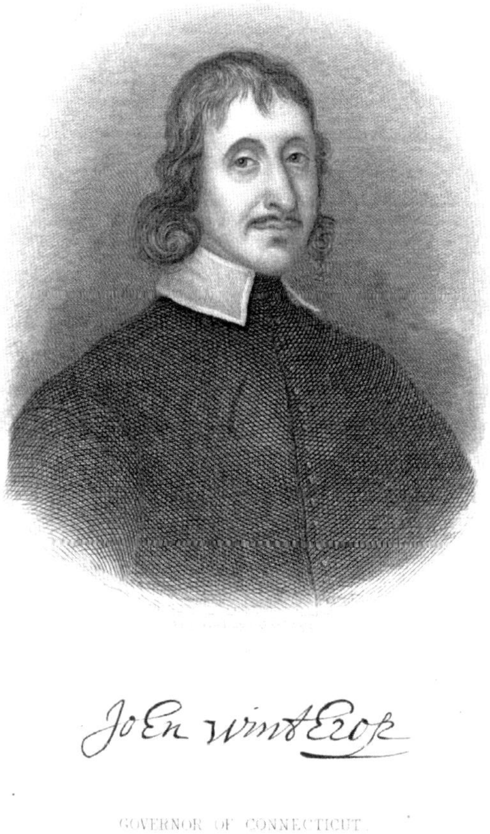

Governor, alchemist and scientist John Winthrop the Younger. *New York Public Library*.

1646, at the very crux of the English Civil War. The craft also found itself at the center of the American and French Revolutions and continued to exert its influence on western governments throughout the twentieth century. The mediators between the Parliamentarians and the Monarchists, between Winthrop the Younger and Charles II, were Freemasons.

Elias Ashmole and Sir Robert Moray, two of John Winthrop's close associates and fellow members of the Royal Society, were the earliest documented Freemasons. While the origins of Freemasonry are obscure and subject to endless speculation, the two earliest documented initiations into the Masonic craft are Robert Moray at the Lodge of Edinburgh on May

20, 1641, and Elias Ashmole, who wrote in his diary that he "was made a Free Mason at Warrington in Lancashire" on October 16, 1646. Both men, throughout the subsequent years, continued to note their Masonic association. Moray was an accomplished military man who fought on the side of the Parliamentarians early in the Civil War, but by 1645, he had come to the support of Charles I. A mathematician, astrologer and occultist, Ashmole was also an artillery officer in the defeated royal army. From its earliest documented history, we find within the ranks of Freemasonry men of influence and accomplishment who sit on opposite sides of political and religious divides. Indeed, with its proscription against the discussion of religion and politics during lodge meetings—a policy that lasts to this day—the Masonic lodge was an essential institution for a nation riven by religious and political dissent.

Ashmole and Moray shared a common interest with John Winthrop in philosophy, magic, alchemy and science—all three men were Fellows of the British Royal Society, with Moray serving as president. They also studied Rosicrucianism, Hermeticism and Kabbalah—subjects that were of great interest to New England's revolutionary Congregational ministers in the eighteenth century, as evidenced by Ezra Stiles's journal entries describing his conversations with the Jewish rabbis and traveling mystics he entertained in his Newport home.

With the restoration of the monarchy after the death of Cromwell in 1660, John Winthrop would have to rely on men such as Ashmole and Moray to smooth his way with the newly crowned Charles II, son of the deposed and executed king. The Colony of Connecticut, which had enjoyed a policy of benign neglect under Cromwell, had reason to fear for its future with the Restoration, particularly because so many of its founders had been sympathetic to, or leaders of, the Parliamentary cause. It was well remembered that Winthrop's father-in-law, Hugh Peters, was one of the signers of Charles I's death warrant. When Winthrop went to England to secure a charter for Connecticut from the new government under Charles II, he knew his mission was an extremely delicate one.

The entirety of Connecticut's claim to legitimacy before 1662 rested on Saybrook's Warwick Patent. Unfortunately, not only was the authenticity of the patent in question, but also a copy of the original could not be produced, and Robert Rich, the Earl of Warwick, who had issued the patent, had been dead four years. In 1662, the only copies of the Warwick Patent were ones that were hastily drafted in that year—supposedly copies of the original, as the one in Winthrop's own hand claims that it is based on the one found

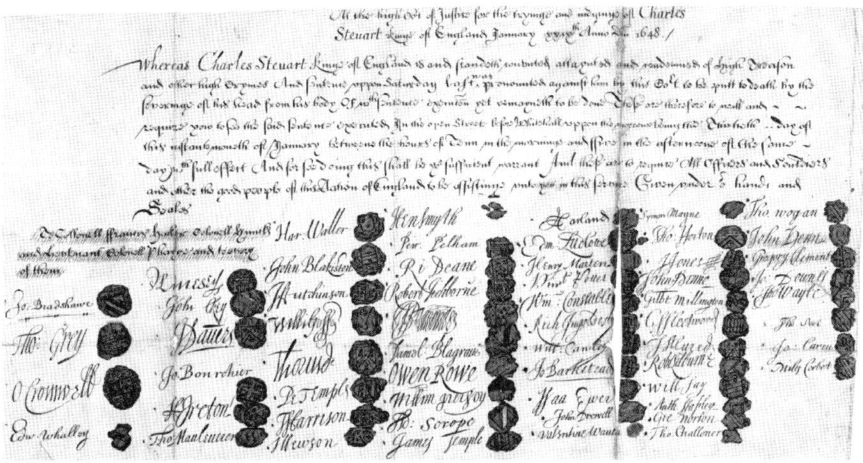

Warrant for the execution of King Charles I. *New York Public Library*.

among George Fenwick's papers. With this thin document in hand, Winthrop appealed to Charles II to grant him a new charter for Connecticut.

Up to this point, Connecticut had operated without royal supervision and conducted itself under the Fundamental Orders, drafted in 1639, which established not only a nearly complete degree of self-governance for the colony but also a remarkable measure of participatory democracy. The Fundamental Orders conspicuously omitted all mention of English authority and, uniquely, in no instance pledged allegiance to the king. Clearly, such an arrangement would not be allowed to persist after the Restoration.

Along with his request for a charter, Winthrop brought with him a declaration of loyalty to present to the king. His entrance into the royal circle was paved by Robert Moray, who also happened to be privy councilor to the king. The king himself also had an interest in alchemy, as recounted by diarist Samuel Pepys, who wrote of visiting the king's alchemical laboratory in the company of Moray.

Winthrop's reputation as an alchemist preceded him to England, with rumors flying that he had discovered the Alkahest, or Philosopher's Stone. Even more importantly, there was no one who knew more about the natural world of New England, the minerals and resources it possessed or how best to access them than Winthrop. Along with his charm and erudition, which were among his many virtues often extolled by contemporaries, Winthrop the Younger could prove very useful to the king in his plan to develop the colonies.

Perhaps Winthrop perused Elias Ashmole's book *Theatrum Chemicum Britannicum*, which the author presented to him as a gift, before meeting with

Charles. Ashmole's *Theatrum* was, in the words of Walter W. Woodward, "a defense of magic as a means of revealing the inner harmonies of the universe." There was certainly some magic at work for Winthrop. When he returned to Connecticut in 1662, John Winthrop carried with him a new royal charter for Connecticut, one that not only legitimized the colony but also remarkably preserved its independence as a self-governing entity, empowered to elect its own general assembly and governor and to make and enforce laws without royal approval or review. It was a charter so amenable to democratic self-government that when the United States declared independence and subsequently adopted the Constitution, Connecticut and Rhode Island were the only states that did not have to adopt new constitutions. The Connecticut Charter of 1662 did not have to be altered or amended and stood as the foundation of Connecticut's government until 1818.

The world of seventeenth-century continental Europe, England and colonial America was striking for its intellectual fervor and the potency of new ideas that were taking hold and laying the foundation for the Age of Enlightenment. Perhaps the most enduring idea to emerge from this era was the notion that the authority of government rests not on the divine right of kings but the consent of the governed. This, among other ideas, is the reason that blood was shed in the English Civil War. Though the monarchy was restored, the notion that the king could rule by royal decree as an absolute monarch had been ultimately defeated; and Charles II made clear that the sovereignty of the three estates would stand inviolate. The consent of the people—a consent fundamental to a government's legitimacy—was to be earned, not coerced.

Perhaps no single writer was more influential in the minds of the English at that time or in the minds of American Patriots during the American Revolution than the philosopher John Locke. Among his formulations taken to heart by Americans was, "All mankind...being all equal and independent, no one ought to harm another in his life, health, liberty, or possessions." Locke argued that the powers of government should be limited, people have intrinsic rights and freedoms, it is the obligation of government to guarantee the well-being of its people and the people have a right to overthrow their government when it no longer protects them or serves their interests.

These ideas, embraced by the founders of the United States and enshrined in the country's political documents, were radical for their age. Locke also argued for religious and intellectual tolerance, and as a member of the Oxford community from 1652 to 1667 and a member of the Royal Society from 1668, Locke was at the epicenter of the revolution of ideas in England.

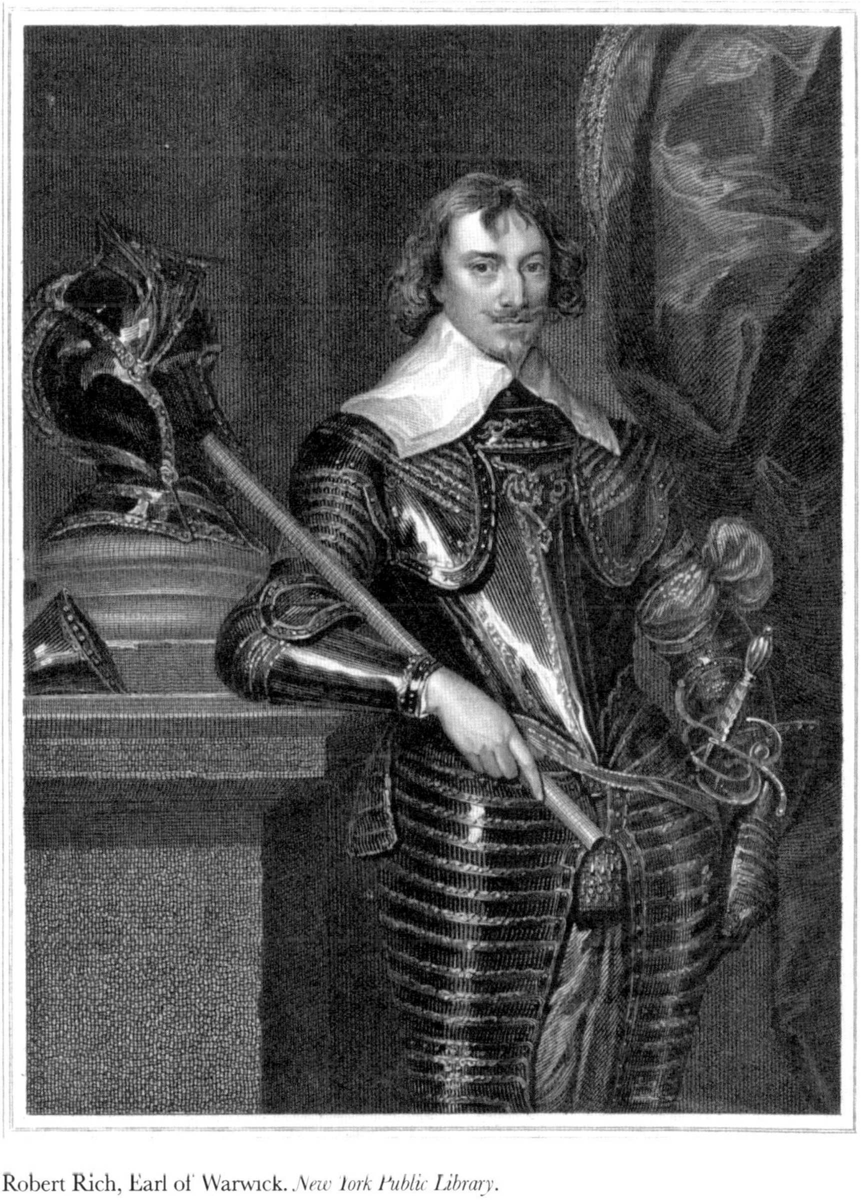

Robert Rich, Earl of Warwick. *New York Public Library.*

Those ideas, flashing across the political landscape of seventeenth-century England, thundered loudly in eighteenth-century America.

When Governor George Fenwick left Saybrook in 1645 to return to England and join Cromwell's forces, he entrusted Saybrook's land east of the Connecticut River to Matthew Griswold. Described variously as

Fenwick's business agent, lawyer, quartermaster and stonecutter, Griswold was probably all of these and more, as the ambitious Renaissance men of this age were often multitalented. Griswold soon moved to this land east of the river and established his home at Black Hall. Along with pioneering families such as the Marvins, Lees, Lays, Elys and Lords, Griswold developed a community that by 1665 was able to petition for independence from the town of Saybrook. Formalized in a document called "The Loving Parting," Lyme was established as a town on February 13 of that year.

While the land became a source of their security and prosperity, perhaps a more potent resource these Lyme citizens carried with them was their worldview—a philosophy that combined hard-won notions of personal self-reliance and political self-determination. In many ways, the Restoration never happened in Lyme. The ideals fought for by the Cromwellians endured. They continued to decide their own affairs at town meeting and elected their own representatives to the general assembly. They exhibited religious tolerance, when they were interested in religion at all. It had been noted at the time, to the consternation of colonial authorities, that it took the citizens of Lyme nearly thirty years to establish a proper church after they were granted the right to do so. In short, the residents of Lyme were answerable only to themselves.

The remarkable independence and stability of Lyme's social and political order throughout the seventeenth and eighteenth centuries made for a culture rich in tradition and memory. Matthew Griswold IV, over a century after his ancestor founded the town, gained fame as a Patriot by walking out of Governor Fitch's office with the Sons of Liberty, not only in protest of the Stamp Act but also as an assurance that the tax would be defied. In time, Griswold would come to be known as Connecticut's "Revolutionary Governor." When Griswold's nephew Samuel Holden Parsons wrote to Samuel Adams in 1773 proposing that the colonies of New England unite, he specifically referred to the New England Confederation of Colonies that had been created by Saybrook's George Fenwick: "I can't but see that our ancestors when they first landed in America were as independent of the Crown or King of Great Britain as if they had never been his subjects."

When George III tugged on the leash of the American colonies, it should have come as no surprise that the citizens of Lyme did not respond with obedience, but defiance and a promise that should he continue to act as tyrant, George III should fear to meet the same fate as Charles I.

Chapter 3

The Great Awakening

How Radical Clerics Shaped a Revolution

In an upstairs room, overlooking the South Green, Lyme's Congregational minister Jonathan Parsons took one last glance in the mirror and adjusted his silver- and gold-laced coat. His wife, Phoebe Griswold Parsons, came up behind him, smiled into the mirror and playfully mussed his hair. Their boys, Marshfield and Samuel Holden, ran through the house excitedly as they prepared for their father's guest to arrive. The great evangelist, the Reverend George Whitefield, was coming to town and would be speaking soon from atop a boulder in Reverend Parsons's own yard. The elders of the congregation had prohibited the radical Whitefield from preaching at the meetinghouse, so Parsons invited him to address the congregation from nature's own pulpit—a glacial erratic placed by the Lord in time immemorial. The great elm trees would serve as the sounding board, the sun pouring through the leaves would be proof of grace and even the songbirds would solemnly withhold their tune and stop to listen to the great divine.

All and sundry came to hear him. Ladies dressed in their finery emerged from their elegant homes, stepping gingerly, arm in arm along the Post Road, their slaves following a few steps behind. Muskrat trappers wrapped in pelts trudged up from the swamps. Teamsters drove their oxen, pulling carts full of farmhands. Fishermen came ashore at the town landings, salt-hayers dropped their scythes and came running and merchants closed up their shops for the day.

The skies turned storm-dark with dust, and the electricity in the air was palpable as multitudes converged on the town green to hear the great man speak. There had never before been such a massive gathering of people in Lyme.

A hush came over the assembled throng as Whitefield began, quietly and in an almost distracted manner. The crowd drew closer and strained to hear his gentle and melodic tones. Gradually, his exhortations grew stronger, as he enumerated the sins of his flock—secrets of the heart, intimate transgressions that his listeners had hidden even from their own consciences: their acts born of doubt and cowardice, falsity masking avarice and deceptions disguising lust. He knew of the seed of the serpent that dwelt within. He showed them the road, the sure path to hellfire that they trod, the fate of eternal damnation that they had sealed with their own hand. Whitefield jumped, screamed, stomped his feet and fell to his knees, trembling, sweat pouring from his brow. In one moment, he could make their hearts soar with hope, then tell an earthy joke, drawing laughter that echoed across the valley, and in the next moment look heavenward, his eyes rolling back in his head and his arms spread wide, bringing the full weight of the Lord's mighty wrath down upon their condemned souls, buckling their knees until they fell down in prayer or reducing them to a miserable state—wailing, inconsolate, sobbing wretches.

But the evangelist did not leave them desolate and forlorn. Just when they could take no more, and the sulfurous fumes of eternal damnation seemed to sting their nostrils, he would offer a ray of light, a glimmer of hope—the promise of salvation. Repent. Accept the Lord and be reborn. You don't need a minister. You don't need a bishop. You don't even need a church.

The date was August 12, 1745. It was the dawn of the Great Awakening in Lyme, and Reverend George Whitefield had arrived. Whitefield's impact on American culture was profound. The esteemed Benjamin Franklin, though famously a Deist, regularly printed Whitefield's sermons and extolled his virtues. Upon hearing Whitefield speak in Philadelphia, Dr. Franklin calculated that the preacher's voice could reach thirty thousand people at a time, and the crowds that gathered to hear him had even exceeded that number in some towns. While freely admitting that he would not be converted, even the clear-eyed and parsimonious Franklin could not help but be moved by the evangelist's performances. In his autobiography, he recalled attending one of Whitefield's events:

I happened soon after to attend one of his Sermons, in the Course of which I perceived he intended to finish with a Collection, and I silently

> *resolved he should get nothing from me. I had in my Pocket a Handful of Copper Money, three or four silver Dollars, and five Pistoles in Gold. As he proceeded I began to soften, and concluded to give the Coppers. Another Stroke of his Oratory made me asham'd of that, and determin'd me to give the Silver; and he finish'd so admirably, that I emptied my Pocket wholly into the Collector's Dish, Gold and all.*

No one had seen a minister carry on like this before or felt the spirit move through them as they did with Whitefield, this open-air preacher without a church. Other firebrands had come before—George Tennent and the famous New Haven divine Jonathan Edwards—but their effect was nothing like this. No one had ever witnessed dour New Englanders behaving in such a frenzy of lamentation and exultation. And with his message of the oppression of damnation and the empowerment of salvation, this firebrand itinerant preacher, who was quickly becoming the most famous and celebrated man in New England, irrevocably split Connecticut's Congregational Church in two. Henceforth, the official church of the colony would have two factions: the New Lights and the Old Lights.

Whitefield's message unnerved civic and religious authorities but struck a chord with a broad cross-section of the public. "Here and there I see a King, and here and there a great man in heaven, but their number is but small," he preached. His message was that salvation was available to all through repentance and rebirth of the spirit, and social position and "good works" would not suffice. It was available to both the meek and the mighty, and indeed, it was more likely for the meek.

Even more annoying to the powers that be was

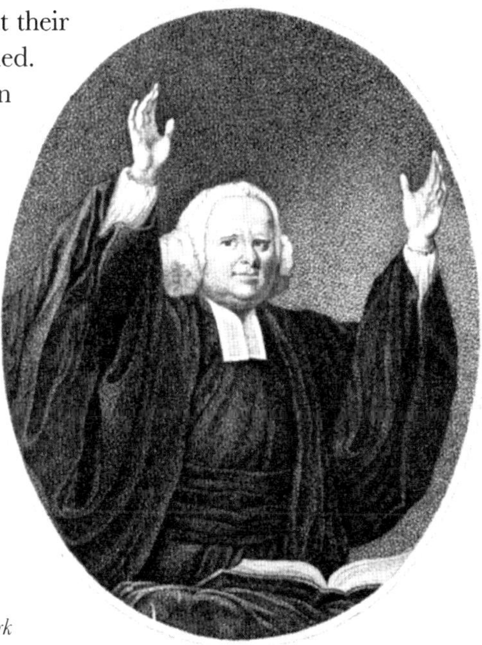

Reverend George Whitefield. *New York Public Library.*

Whitefield's welcoming attitude toward black slaves and Native Americans at his events. In his view, salvation was equally available to the slave and the master. Not that Whitefield was an abolitionist—far from it. In fact, he was a strong supporter of slavery and often preached biblical justifications for it. But at the same time, he exhorted slave masters to treat their servants well and condemned those who were abusive. While he considered the institution of slavery to be biblically ordained, slaves were nevertheless equally human and capable of salvation. A freed slave in Philadelphia who heard Whitefield speak was converted, not so much by the message, but by the sight of sweat pouring from the preacher's brow. Not only did it remind him of the way he'd sweated while toiling in the cane fields of Montserrat, but it also was the first time he had ever witnessed a white man do so. To him, it was proof of Whitefield's sincerity.

Nowhere did the Great Awakening cause a greater sensation than in eastern Connecticut. Long a bastion of sectarians, dissenters, eccentrics and the irreligious, by the 1740s the colony was more concerned with mercantile interests than matters of the spirit. Church fathers bemoaned the lack of devotion among parishioners, increasing materialism and an even more troubling tendency toward hedonism. Ezra Stiles wrote that the citizens of eastern Connecticut "are of a very mixt and uncertain character as to religion" and "Exhorters, Itinerants, [and] Separate Meetings rose in that part."

It was a region that experienced an economic boom after 1690, especially between 1730 and 1760, when the population of the colony tripled. Growth was focused on the eastern part of the state, where a rising class of tradesmen, merchants and farmers prospered with the opening of trade with the West Indies.

In Lyme, self-reliance and industriousness were generally more prized than devotion. Even before the church's formal establishment in 1693, there were dissenters. Elizabeth, the daughter of Matthew Griswold I, married John Rogers, founder of the controversial Rogerine Quakers. Rogers, considered a "freethinker and heretic," came into open conflict with his friends and neighbors by 1675, when he founded a separatist Sabbatarian church in New London.

In 1727, Valentine Wightman, who founded Connecticut's first Baptist church, in nearby Groton, engaged in a debate in Lyme with traditionalist Reverend John Bulkley concerning freedom of religion and dissent. An account of the debate, published by Timothy Green under the title *An Impartial Account of a Late Debate at Lyme in the Colony of Connecticut*, reports that one of the issues heatedly discussed was whether "to Baptize Women Naked is an immodest Action and a Incitement to Uncleaness." That practice, which had come into vogue, was defended by its practitioners as biblically sound, while the more modest among Lyme's citizens complained that baptizing adult men and women together, naked, only encouraged lasciviousness and adultery. Also debated were the issues of taxation without representation and separation of church and state. Separatists argued that their taxes should not support the officially sanctioned Congregational Church, and it was this division among Christian sects that first gave rise to the notion that the roles of government and religion must be completely separate if one was to guarantee the legitimacy of the former and freedom of the latter. All of the town's leaders were present at this debate, including Matthew Griswold IV. By 1755, nearly one-third of Lyme's residents were "dissenters"—that is, Baptists, Quakers or those unaffiliated with any church at all.

The Congregational Church itself was in turmoil. As the officially sanctioned church of the colony, religious questions took on a political hue, and political dissent played out in the pulpit and the pew. Dissent in theocratic governments takes on a religious character out of necessity, as it is often the most potent means of expression. The Great Awakening loosened up those modes of expression. Lyme's Reverend Jonathan Parsons described the effects of one of his New Light sermons on his congregation in April 1744:

> *While I was preaching—I observed many of the assembly in tears, and heard many crying out in very great bitterness of the soul….Alas! I'm undone! I'm undone! O my sins! How shall I escape the damnation of hell?*

He also noted further visceral reactions:

> *The joints of their loins were loosed, and their knees smote one against another. Great numbers cried aloud in the anguish of their souls. Several stout men fell as though a cannon has been discharged and a ball had made its way through their hearts. Some young women were thrown into hysteric fits.*

The reserved denizens of Lyme had never behaved in such a way before, at least not in public. But this was a new form of religious expression, and the congregation was encouraged to cry out and participate. Kicking, shouting, screaming, writhing and fainting were all signs of a true convert. Whitefield had even said that ministers who preached in the old, formal style were "dead" and "unconverted." Not everyone agreed. When Alexander Hamilton came through Lyme on August 27, 1744, he referred to the New Lights as "clowns." But, while

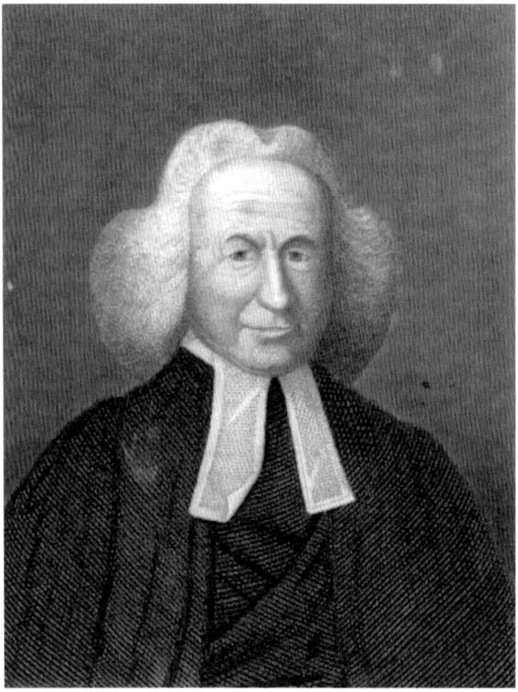

Reverend Jonathan Parsons. *New York Public Library.*

the intense fervor of the converted soon cooled, the New Lights had made their mark. The lessons of the church meeting would soon be carried over to the town meeting. Voices that had once been silent in political affairs would soon be emboldened to cry out.

The Great Awakening in Connecticut had a political character from the outset. Reverend Jonathan Parsons's embrace of it was not only a question of preaching style and doctrinal points—he also very early on rejected the "Saybrook Platform," which had been passed by the colonial legislature in 1705 establishing a central authority in the Congregational Church. The New Lights rejected all such hierarchy. There would be no earthly authority above the congregation. Ministers need not be approved by religious officeholders appointed to do so but could be chosen by the congregation itself and confirmed by a "laying of hands."

The separation of church and state began in eastern Connecticut out of necessity. The colony could not survive and prosper if its civic life was rife with religious factionalism. It seemed there were as many opinions on spiritual dogma as there were citizens, and these disagreements were bad for business. In fact, these inheritors of Cromwell's project were like-minded in civic affairs: they were in favor of free trade, free thought and free enterprise. Above all, they were in favor of self-governance and self-determination in political affairs. They were not about to take orders from church authorities and unelected royal ministers from across the Atlantic. In matters both spiritual and civic, the citizens of Lyme would be dictated to by no one and did not need anyone's permission to act.

The New Lights of the Congregational Church became a political party with the general assembly's passage of the Itinerancy Act in 1742. This act prohibited ministers from preaching outside their own churches without permission and also prevented unaffiliated ministers or those not properly ordained from traveling through the colony and setting up shop at will: no more wild-eyed preachers roaming the countryside and exhorting from atop boulders, whipping up the rabble.

The supporters of the Itineracy Act were the political and religious establishment: the Old Lights, centered mostly in the western part of the state, who were tired of these nobodies challenging their theology and, even worse, their legitimacy. What the Old Lights didn't count on, however, is how deeply the Great Awakening had shaken the eastern part of the state and how profoundly it had touched not only the disaffected but also the elite. Lyme's most prominent family, the Griswolds, were drawn into the church by the Great Awakening and Parsons's ministry. Jonathan Parsons married Phoebe Griswold, Matthew Griswold IV's sister. Matthew Griswold was not only the heir of the town's founder, he was also the leading attorney in the region and in 1751 became Lyme's elected representative to the general assembly.

The power brokers in Hartford were seemingly unaware of this rebellion brewing in their backyard. Matthew Griswold was a trusted stalwart of the established order and, one would think, an avatar of traditionalism and continuity. But Griswold was also a New Light, as were most of Lyme's leading citizens. Reverend Jonathan Parsons would soon prove too strong a drink for starchy, reserved Lyme, but his replacement, Stephen Johnson, was just as committed to New Light philosophy and politically every bit as incendiary. These men—Parsons, Johnson and Griswold—are a direct link between the New Lights of the Congregational Church and the Sons of Liberty, who would be catalysts of the American Revolution.

The political evolution of the New Lights was marked by a blend of philosophy and self-interest. It was no accident that these men of eastern Connecticut, whose ancestors had been followers of Cromwell, took a dim view of being told what to do by political or religious ministers not of their choosing. One of the rifts that further defined the New Lights as a political party was the question of the Susquehanna Company. In the early 1760s, the Susquehanna Company was founded by a group of speculators who, cobbling together newly signed Indian deeds and the old Warwick Patent, laid claim to lands along Pennsylvania's Susquehanna River for the citizens of Connecticut.

The Old Lights of the western part of the colony were opposed to the enterprise. These were large landholders, and Connecticut's population explosion was good for their bottom line, as real estate values soared. They were opposed to opening up new lands because it would not only depress real estate values but also draw attention from London should the Crown be called in to mediate a dispute between the colonies of Pennsylvania and Connecticut.

In the east, however, where population growth was concentrated and landholdings smaller, the Susquehanna Company seemed like a good opportunity, not only for relocation of a burgeoning and crowded agrarian class, but also as an investment for the newly prosperous merchant class.

The Susquehanna Company sold shares to farmers and businessmen alike, and its prime supporters were two men who would be among eastern Connecticut's most significant players in the American Revolution: Son of Liberty John Durkee and Lyme's Major General Samuel Holden Parsons, son of Reverend Jonathan. Perhaps it was historically no coincidence that the two Old Lights most remembered as opposing the Susquehanna Company were Governor Thomas Fitch and Stamp Act enforcer Jared Ingersoll.

This was a period when English subjects were becoming American citizens. The lines were blurry and irregularly drawn, and the lay of the land was quickly changing. One could be at ease in the seat of power one minute and have one's life threatened for treason the next. This was the position that Jared Ingersoll unexpectedly found himself in on September 17, 1765. At the time, Ingersoll was one of Connecticut's comfortable political grandees. He made a name for himself at Yale in 1742 by opposing the Great Awakening. As a young disciple of the Old Lights, he was rewarded with an appointment as Connecticut's agent to Great Britain in 1758. When he returned to New Haven in 1761, Ingersoll was forced to confront a new reality: the New Lights had taken control of the lower house of the general assembly.

Ingersoll was well connected. What could these rogue New Light assemblymen from the eastern swamplands have on his patrons, such as British treasury secretary Thomas Whatley? Ingersoll was a native son of Connecticut, a Yale graduate and an intimate of the British court and Parliament. But when Whatley and British prime minister George Grenville were searching for ways to replenish the British treasury, which had been drained by the long and costly war with France, they looked to the newly prosperous colonial backwater that was America. Once the province of what they deemed savages, dissenters, visionaries, misfits, dreamers and malcontents, by the eighteenth century, America had become an economic engine that, while it reflected glory upon the Crown, did not provide enough revenue to augment the Crown jewels. Thus, Ingersoll's friend Whatley, along with Grenville, devised the Stamp Act to raise revenues for the British treasury. Benjamin Franklin thought it a fine idea and a very sensible one at that. He encouraged Ingersoll to accept the commission to become the collector of the Stamp Tax. Ingersoll was uncomfortable with the role and thus needed Dr. Franklin's persuasion. Britain had already passed two resolutions that were very unpopular in Connecticut: one in 1763 constricting trade with non-English ports and the Sugar Act of 1764. Ingersoll could see why the colonists were opposed, but as a loyal British subject, he could see the Crown's side as well and submitted to upholding the acts.

In Lyme, this was the moment that the war against Britain was declared in the hearts of the citizenry. It was a war of ideas that the Patriots of the land had won in the hearts and minds of their neighbors—now it had only to be proved in battle against Mother England. This empire, in the words of the revolutionary Reverend Jonathan Parsons, was "a cruel mother, deaf to the voice of liberty and right." Stephen Johnson would write even sharper words against the empire. His words would be carried like lightning up and down the Boston Post Road and inflame the citizenry to revolution.

Chapter 4

Stephen Johnson and the Stamp Act

You have, my dear friends, as good a right to your Privileges as Britain have of theirs and you have as dearly bought them. If you should not do all that you can, to preserve that inestimable Jewel of Liberty, your Posterity, in the anguish of their Souls, will load your Memories with the bitterest Reproaches. But I know you will. Remember, O my friends, the Laws, the Rights, the generous Plan of Power deliver'd down, From Age to Age, by your Forefathers, Ne'r ever let it Perish in your Hands, but piously transmit it to your Children.

—Reverend Stephen Johnson

So wrote Lyme's Reverend Stephen Johnson under the pseudonym "Addison" on September 6, 1765, in a letter published in Timothy Green's *New London Gazette* answering Connecticut stamp collector Jared Ingersoll's justification for the Stamp Act, penned under the name "Civis." The following week, on September 13, Johnson's rhetoric grew hot: "But let not Stampmen deceive themselves—the people are not yet so bewitched to trade and property, as for the sake of that, valuable as it is, to part with their INVALUABLE RIGHTS AND LIBERTIES." He goes on to address Ingersoll, a Connecticut native son, an Old Light in the employ of the Crown, directly:

> *Are the people of Connecticut so particularly devoted to you, a NATIVE—whom they have oblig'd and honor'd…do you suppose, so well affected to YOU, more than to any man, as to be willing to receive what they take to be their quieting dose at your beloved hands?*

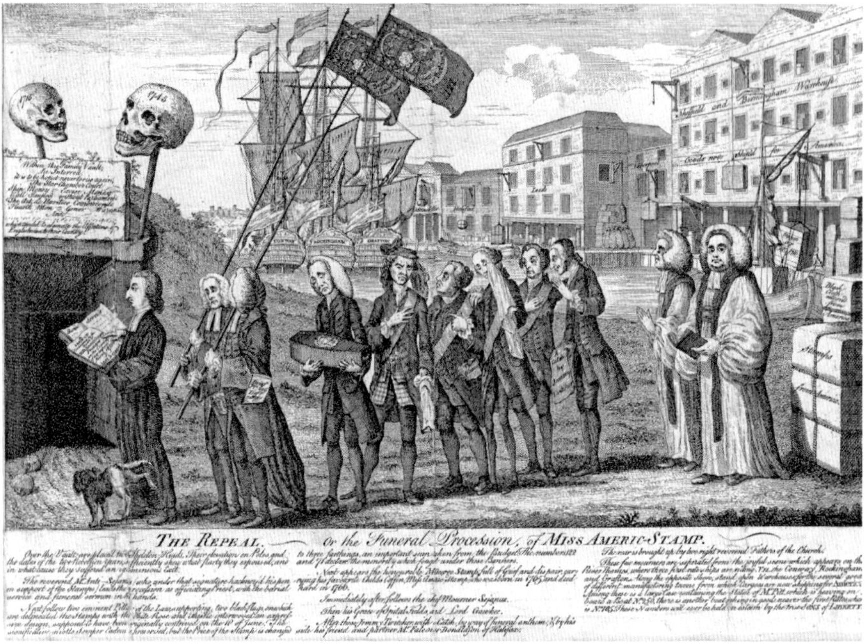

"Death of Miss Americ-stamp" cartoon. *New York Public Library.*

Four days later, Jared Ingersoll had been hounded from his office in New Haven and was on his way to Hartford to receive council from his cohorts, the Old Lights of the upper house of Connecticut's legislature, and to get his orders from Governor Thomas Fitch. But Ingersoll was waylaid in Wethersfield by a band of five hundred Sons of Liberty, who promised that the Sons of Liberty would receive either the stampman's resignation or his life, purchased at the expense of a noose strung from the tree beneath which he stood. Ingersoll surveyed the bough from which he would be hanged; noted the number of the crowd, many of whom he knew personally; and promptly submitted his resignation, including a threefold "huzzah" to American liberty.

For the Patriots of Lyme, the American Revolution was fought and won on that day. The only question was how much time and what expense of blood and treasure would be necessary to secure that victory for their posterity.

What the British and the Old Light Tory sympathizers didn't know was that the New Lights of eastern Connecticut, though divided in religious squabbles and distracted by immediate concerns of commerce, were united in the cause of independence and liberty. The blood of their predecessors, who had beheaded King Charles I, still flowed mightily like a river through their bodies as they prepared to take on the monarchy and royal ministers once again.

The resistance had begun a year earlier with the Sugar Act, which would have strangled the commerce of Connecticut's coastal towns. The act was openly defied, in both letter and practice. The Stamp Act was an even greater insult to the colony's sovereignty and would levy an onerous tax on colonists without their consent (a tax not levied on residents of Britain proper) but also put Connecticut's newspapers (such as New London's *Gazette* and Hartford's *Courant*) out of business. This insulted merchant and publisher alike, and the union of these aggrieved parties would prove fatal to the Stamp Act in short order.

Stephen Johnson and his fellow Patriots in Lyme, including his neighbor and the town's leading merchant John McCurdy, objected to the Stamp Act from the outset. Passed by Parliament on March 22, 1765, the Stamp Act was designed to raise revenue for the British treasury by compelling Americans to purchase stamps and affix them to all of their paper documents, including wills, contracts, ship's papers, licenses, newspapers and even playing cards. The cost of the stamp was not negligible; a newspaper publisher would have to pay a penny for each four-page copy of the newspaper and two shillings for each ad. By comparison, the average price for a yearly newspaper subscription in 1765 was between six and eight shillings. For the American press, the Stamp Act was not just an inconvenience—it was a death sentence.

Even those who could afford to pay the tax found it objectionable on moral and philosophical grounds. This was quite simply taxation without representation. It was an act dictated by the British Parliament, a legislative body in which America had no voice and held no seat. While the English insisted that the Americans were "virtually" represented in Parliament, Johnson called this "a mysterious representation, and of most uncertain Signification." In his September 6 letter, he goes on to say:

> *If the British Parliament have right to impose a Stamp Tax, they have a right to lay on us a Poll Tax, a Land Tax, a Malt Tax, a Cyder Tax, a Window Tax, a Smoke Tax, and why not Tax us for the Light of the Sun, the Air we Breathe, and the Ground we are Buried in? If they have Right to deny us the Privilege of Tryals by Juries, they have as good a Right to deny us any Tryals at all, and to vote away our Estates and Lives at Pleasure.*

Ezra Stiles, the Congregational minister at Newport and later president of Yale, was a close friend of fellow Yale alum Stephen Johnson. As ecclesiastical

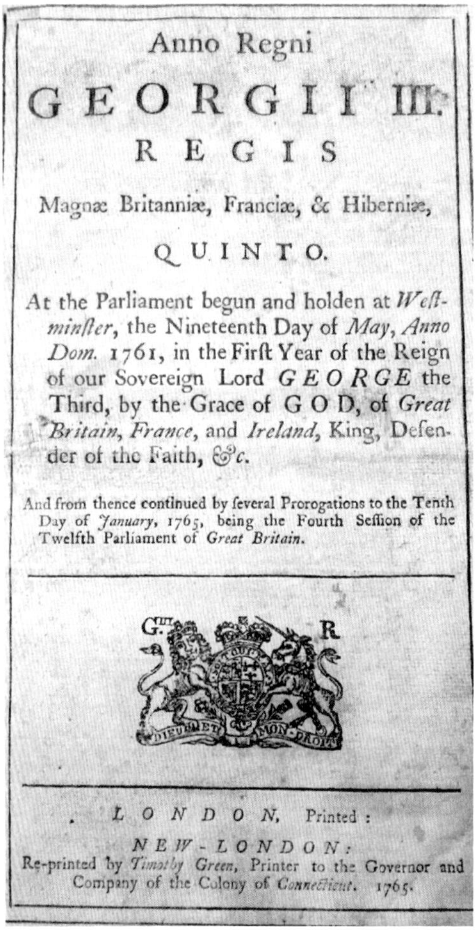

Anno Regni
GEORGII III.
REGIS
Magnæ Britanniæ, Franciæ, & Hiberniæ,
QUINTO.

At the Parliament begun and holden at *Weſt-minſter*, the Nineteenth Day of *May*, *Anno Dom.* 1761, in the Firſt Year of the Reign of our Sovereign Lord *GEORGE* the Third, by the Grace of GOD, of *Great Britain*, *France*, and *Ireland*, King, Defender of the Faith, *&c.*

And from thence continued by ſeveral Prorogations to the Tenth Day of *January*, 1765, being the Fourth Seſſion of the Twelfth Parliament of *Great Britain*.

LONDON, Printed:
NEW-LONDON:
Re-printed by *Timothy Green*, Printer to the Governor and Company of the Colony of *Connecticut*. 1765.

The Stamp Act, printed by Timothy Green, New London, 1765. *New London County Historical Society.*

and family matters frequently took Stiles from Newport to New Haven, he often visited Johnson in Lyme, and when Stiles was chosen to be president of Yale, Johnson was selected to relay the news to him. It is through Stiles that we have confirmation that the *Gazette* letters of autumn 1765 were indeed the work of Johnson's pen, and it is from Stiles's correspondence of April 16, 1765, that we discover that Johnson singled out the date of the Stamp Act's passage thus: "[F]rom this time, says Mr. Johnson, date the Slavery of the Colonies."

Indeed, one of the marks of Johnson's writing against the Stamp Act is his use of the word "slavery," or "inslavement," in describing its effect on the colonists. Ironically, John McCurdy, the man who brought Johnson's essays to New London's Timothy Green for publication, was himself a slaveholder. The very same issues of New London's *Gazette* that carried Johnson's jeremiads against the "inslaving" nature of the Stamp Act also carried advertisements offering rewards for the return of runaway slaves. Printer Timothy Green inserted an ad in the November 8, 1765 issue that announced: "To Be SOLD. A likely Negro Boy, about 13 Years of Age, has been in the Country about twelve Months, speaks pretty good English. Enquire of the Printer."

The irony of wealthy merchants, ministers and publishers decrying the Stamp Act as slavery while they themselves held actual slaves, brokered the sale of slave children or tacitly condoned such practices was not lost on forward-thinking Patriots of the day. By the time of the Declaration of Independence, the question of slavery would be front and center in the debate of who we would be as a nation and how we were to conduct ourselves. The legal and moral implications of slavery were apparent in the mid-eighteenth century and discussed openly. It was not an institution that was unconsciously adhered to as a simple ancient relic of the past or an accepted economic arrangement—slavery was debated and deliberately reconfirmed at the nation's founding, despite vehement opposition from patriotic luminaries such as John Adams and the Marquis de Lafayette. Indeed, by 1776, the Congregational Church itself had been shamed into opposing slavery by virtue of Newport's Reverend Samuel Hopkins, who wrote the influential pamphlet *A Dialogue Concerning the Slavery of the Africans; Shewing It to Be the Duty and Interest of the American States to Emancipate All the African Slaves*, published by Judah Spooner in Norwich. In this pamphlet, Hopkins heroically and patriotically called the Sons of Liberty on the carpet, writing, "[A]nd behold the Sons of Liberty, oppressing and tyrannizing over many thousands of poor blacks who have as good a claim to liberty as themselves."

While the question of slavery would remain unresolved and become an ominous contradiction in the American psyche that would tear the nation apart one hundred years later in a horrific civil war whose implications continue to resonate to the present day, the colonists of eastern Connecticut were united in the notion of autonomy, self-government and opposition to the dictates of Britain's Parliament. Ezra Stiles wrote on October 23 that three-quarters of Connecticut's men were "ready to take up their Arms for their Liberties: to which they no more question their Right than to their Lands." On November 1, 1765, the day the Stamp Act took effect, Stephen Johnson wrote in the *New London Gazette*: "O my Country. My dear distressed country! For you I have wrote; for you I daily mourn, and to save your invaluable Rights and Freedom, I would willingly die."

The timeline of resistance to the Stamp Act is a dramatic illustration of the readiness and willingness of Connecticut citizens to defend their sovereignty, even to the point of death, and the steadfast resolve in the moral and philosophical certitude of their cause. The British did themselves no favor by delaying the implementation of the Stamp Act. While the act was passed in March 1765, it would not take effect until November of that year. It was a period that the British ministers thought could be used to persuade colonists to adhere to the revenue-raising measure and to enlist American-born Loyalists to support the tax and convince their fellow colonists of its necessity. In reality, the only thing the seven-month waiting period did was give colonists time to

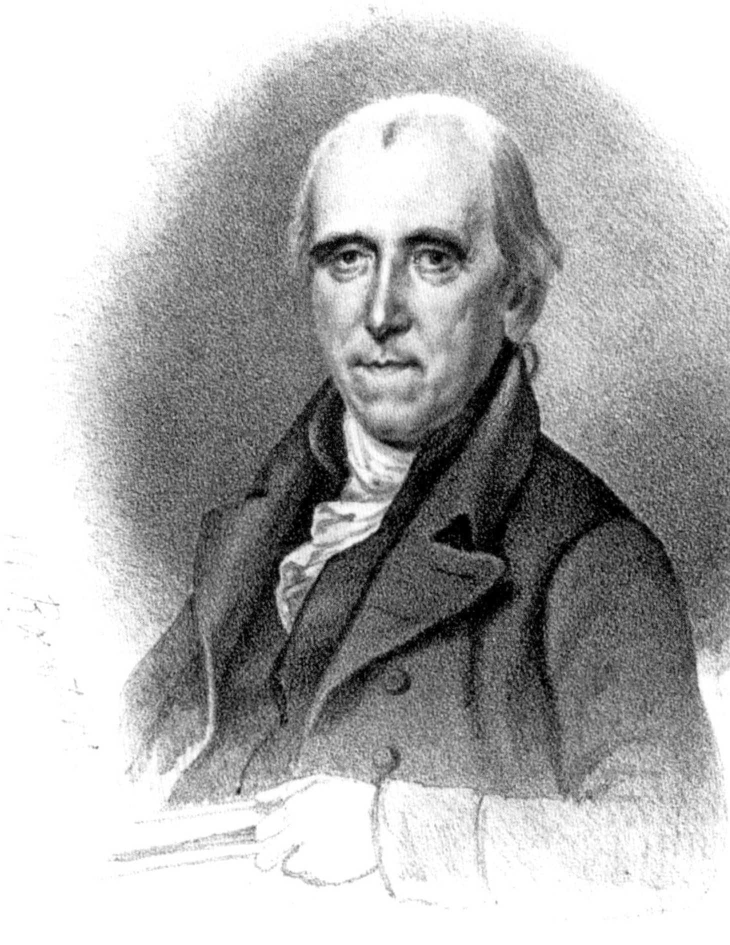

Stamp tax collector Jared Ingersoll. *New York Public Library*.

organize, both politically and militarily. By the time the question of enactment was on the table, even the landing of the stamps themselves at the harbor was considered an act of war. It was a war against an empire in which the colonists of Connecticut were fully prepared to engage.

Throughout the spring and summer of 1765, Americans petitioned to have the Stamp Act repealed, but their pleas were not heard. On September 6, Reverend Stephen Johnson's first letter opposing the Stamp Act appeared in the *New London Gazette*. In that same issue, an account of a mock trial held in Lyme also appears. The trial was of one J---d Stampman, Esq., who was being "indicted by the good People of this Colony" and tried "before the Protectors of Liberty." The charges against Stampman made clear that he was a thinly veiled stand-in for Jared Ingersoll. The particulars against him included "being mov'd thereto by the instigation of the Devil, he did on the 29th of Sept 1764, kill and murder one of his own Brethren" and "he did, on the 5th day of June 1765, enter into a Confederacy with some other evil minded, wicked, and malicious persons to kill and destroy his own Mother, Americana." September 29, 1764, referred to the implementation of the Sugar Act, which charged the colonists three pence per gallon of molasses imported into the Americas, payable to the king. The act also set up admiralty courts in Nova Scotia to try maritime cases, thus circumventing all of America's institutions of jurisprudence, and restricted the importation of staples such as wines and cloth, subjecting them to onerous duties and forcing all trade through British ports. The Sugar Act was the first British act of Parliament that was met with widespread derision and disobedience along the Connecticut shore. Not until the Volstead Act banned alcohol in 1920 would Connecticut again so cheerfully and blatantly disregard the law and its enforcers in such a blithe manner.

The second indictment reveals just how far relations between Britain and America had deteriorated in the past year. While the Sugar Act was willfully disregarded and barely enforced, the Stamp Act carried with it not only an onerous tax on the business of the colony—and of the free press, which disseminated the information that was the lifeblood of the open economy—it also promised the threat of enforcement at the hand of the British army and mercenaries, which the British Parliament intended to land on American shores to ensure conformity.

This was an act of war against the protestors in America. Little did Britain know that the loud voices of their Loyalist sycophants betrayed the scarcity of their number and it was, in fact, the protesting Patriots, whose voices they would not hear, who were a committed and organized majority that, not cowed by the threat of war, would be prepared to rise to the challenge and emerge victorious.

The date ascribed to the second indictment, June 5, 1765, was the day that Jared Ingersoll accepted his position as stamp collector.

Stampman's trial, sponsored by Lyme's Sons of Liberty and, it was said, presided over by Lyme's chief magistrate Matthew Griswold IV, ended with a conviction and a sentence served. This broke the fourth wall of the political theater that was this mock trial. When Stampman was sentenced to death by hanging from a "Gallows erected at least 50 feet high" and his dead body "buried at the meeting of three Roads," with a memorial erected so that the "infamy of the Crime" would be "perpetuated to after Generations," it not only served as a symbolic gesture, but it was also a direct warning to Jared Ingersoll as to the nature of his fate should he persist in his Loyalist ways.

The trial was held in Lyme on August 29, 1765, hard on the heels of the first such trial held by Boston's Sons of Liberty, which counted Samuel and John Adams among their number, on August 14, and Newport's trial on the twenty-seventh.

The account of Lyme's mock trial was most likely written by Stephen Johnson on September 3 and published in the *Gazette* on September 6. Within two weeks, on September 17, Ingersoll would be met by five hundred Sons of Liberty on his way to Hartford and be given a choice: his resignation or his life. Resistance was futile. In addition to the five hundred men on horseback he was facing, another contingent from the shoreline that included Lyme's Sons of Liberty was also on the way. Though Ingersoll demurred in New Haven that he might not have had the authority to resign, on this occasion, he wisely decided that he did indeed have the right to tender his resignation and did so two days later, on the nineteenth. His resignation, complete with Masonic phrasing, is as follows:

> *I do hereby Promise; that I will never receive any Stamp Papers which may arrive from Europe, in consequence of an Act lately passed in the British Parliament; nor officiate in any Manner as Stamp Master, or Distributor of Stamps within this Colony of Connecticut, either directly or indirectly. And I do hereby Notify all the Inhabitants of this His Majesty's Colony (notwithstanding the said Office has lately been committed to me) not to apply to me ever hereafter for any such Stamp'd Papers, hereby Declaring, that I do Resign said Office, and execute these Presents of my own free Will and Accord, without any Equivocation or Mental Reservation. On Witness whereof I have hereunto set my Hand.—J. Ingersoll*

With this resignation, the New Lights of eastern Connecticut and the Sons of Liberty, through their unity and power in numbers, gained their first concrete victory in their resistance to English rule. While the man they had taken on was only Connecticut's stamp collector, the colonists, though they professed to being loyal subjects, were fully prepared to take on the English king himself rather than submit to a tax they considered unconstitutional.

Johnson's account of J---d Stampman's mock trial in Lyme was marked with barbed humor, elevated by symbolic references to Shakespeare's *Julius Caesar*, the English Civil War and the Cromwellians. Among the judges were Cato, a noble opponent of Caesar, who in Shakespeare's play declares himself "a foe to tyrants, and my country's friend." Brutus is, of course, well known as one of Caesar's assassins. Johnson also lists John Hampden as council for the prosecution. Hampden was one of the leading figures in the English Civil War and first gained fame through his refusal to pay ship money—a tax levied on property owners by Charles I without Parliament's consent. His resistance is seen as the beginning of the civil war and the struggle between the monarch and Parliament, and Hampden remained a hero and role model for American Patriots. In case anyone missed this symbolism, Johnson's writing in the *Gazette* on October 11, 1765, put a finer point on it. Responding to threats that Britain would land a military force of fifteen thousand men at Boston to enforce the Stamp Act, Johnson writes:

> *But do not such sycophants know that a standing army for such purposes in a time of peace, is most contrary to the spirit of the British constitution? That it is most dangerous to the liberties of a free people, that Rome—France, and many others—lost their Liberties by it. Have they forgot how it alarmed our nation, and the effects of it in the reigns of Charles the first and James the second?*

After reminding the British of Charles's fate, he goes on to warn of a new civil war:

> *May not such preposterous officious impolicy send us a Caesar, to break off our connection to Great Britain, and set up as a protector of the liberties of the colonies? Or may it not plunge us here and at home, into a bloody civil war, the damage of which to the nation, a hundred thousand hireling scribblers could not countervail?*

He concludes by saying:

> *What is Sport to them is DEATH to us. For the moment but 300 Regulars are imposed upon Americans for such a purpose, our Liberty is lost—we are in fact under a military government, which is no government—'tis horrid tyranny, and one of the worst sort—And who needs a moment to determine whether it is protection or distruction such scribblers drive at.*

On November 1, the date the Stamp Act was to take effect, Governor Thomas Fitch called in his council to administer an oath, whereby he would proclaim his fidelity to Britain and obligation to enforce the act. In a move that Fitch considered treasonous but the New Lights and Sons of Liberty thought patriotic and necessary to upholding Connecticut's freedom, a majority of the governor's councilors walked out on him and refused to administer the oath. Among them was Lyme's Matthew Griswold IV, who sided with the colony's most prominent and confirmed Sons of Liberty, Jonathan Trumbull and Israel Putnam.

On the same day, Johnson wrote in the *Gazette*:

> *For if we may judge by the experience of past ages, a free people will not continue under tyranny or military government any longer than 'til they can reassume their rightful freedom. Such a measure would far more likely produce a distrust and hatred, terminating as hopeless, desperate, irreconcilable enmity, than any good consequence; Nor can the forcing the act fail of producing great tumults and violences in England, as well as America, when their trade, their woolens and other manufactures fail for want of market.*

Johnson makes clear that the Stamp Act, if not repealed, meant war. Elsewhere he wrote:

> *If they must be absolute masters, and we wretched slaves, who may neither buy nor sell—nor have any legal securities or remedies, of defense of Life, Liberty, and Property, but upon their terms, to be newly fixed for us as oft as they see fit. Good God! Where is the constitution! What a slender tenure this, for Englishmen to hold all their privileges by! As the result of all, Do not these measures tend to a very fatal Civil War?*

The Connecticut newspapers were openly defiant. The *Connecticut Courant* in Hartford initially suspended publication rather than submit to carrying stamps, and when it defiantly returned, the paper replaced its masthead with a skull and crossbones. The *New London Gazette* continued business as usual, refusing to be stamped, and thumbed its nose at the act on November 15, 1765, by replacing its masthead with one that simply read: "Liberty and Property, and NO STAMPS." After Johnson's first two letters in September, the *Gazette* turned its entire front page over to him for the next few weeks, and his writings were reprinted in newspapers throughout the colonies.

Resistance to the act was not entirely spontaneous. The Sons of Liberty were in communication from Boston to New York, and representatives

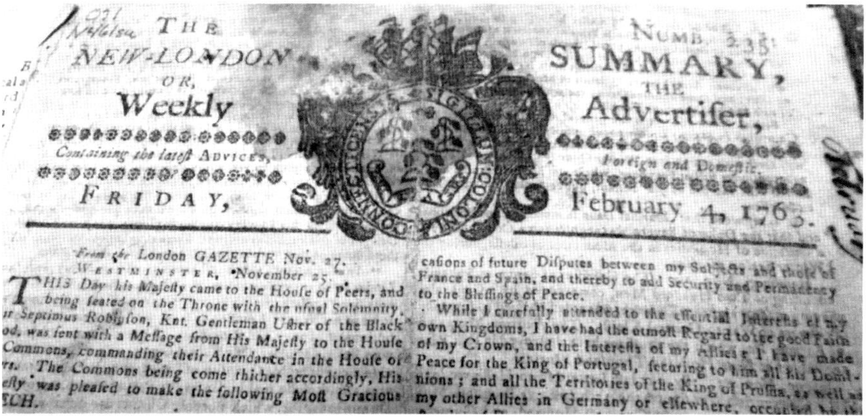

The *New London Summary* (later the *Connecticut Gazette*) masthead with the Connecticut seal, 1763. *New London County Historical Society.*

of nine colonies met in June 1765 at the Stamp Act Congress held in New York City, where they agreed to collective action. The agreement was taken one step further on December 10, 1765, when the Connecticut and New York Sons of Liberty met in New London and agreed to come to the defense of any colony that was attacked by Britain should the Crown seek to enforce the act. Their resolution, as published in the December 27 issue of the *Gazette*, asserts that they agree "to march with the utmost dispatch, at their own proper costs and expense, on the first proper notice (which must be signified to them by at least six of the Sons of Liberty) with their whole force if required….to the relief of those that shall, are, or may be in danger from the Stamp Act." With this agreement, the two colonies agreed to unity and coordinated military action against Britain. Preparations had begun for war.

Connecticut's general assembly had already approved the Stamp Act Congress's resolves opposing the act, but by the end of 1765, individual towns were calling meetings and issuing resolutions of open defiance. Lyme issued its own resolves at the beginning of 1766, which defined its philosophical opposition to the acts and also justified threats to those who supported it. The resolves are considered to be the work of Stephen Johnson, and indeed, the language has a familiar ring. In part, it reads:

> *At a meeting of the respectable populace held at Lyme, in the County of New London, on the 2nd Tuesday of January 1766, the following Resolves were unanimously agreed to and to be inserted in the* New-London Gazette, *vis.*

> *That we have an inviolable right by the God of nature as well as by the English constitution, (Which is unalienable even by ourselves) to those privileges and immunities which by the execution of the Stamp Act we shall be forever stript and deprived.*
>
> *That we are unalterably fixt to defend our aforesaid Rights and Immunities, against every just attack by every lawful way and mean.*
>
> *That our aversion and threats to any person in publick character or other in the colony, is and shall be only on account and according as they are more or less engaged, and active directly or indirectly, to carry into execution the detestable and oppressive Stamp Act which would be an indelible stain to England's glory, and perpetual chains to American Liberty.*

The Resolves go on to appoint Major Durkee of Norwich to correspond with the Sons of Liberty in neighboring colonies, and Lyme's Sons of Liberty are further instructed to keep a "vigilant watch: for the *Cygnet* Man of War, which is carrying the Stamped Papers" and "hovering on our coasts," prevent the landing of those papers and confiscate them if possible.

The appointment of Major Durkee was significant, as he was not only the leader of the Connecticut Sons of Liberty but also the driving force behind the Susquehanna Company. The Lyme Resolves also use the same language, derived from John Locke and other Enlightenment philosophers, that Thomas Jefferson would later use in drafting the Declaration of Independence.

The concepts of inalienable rights, no taxation without representation, separation of church and state, the inviolable sanctity of life, liberty and property—these had been part of Lyme's political orientation at least a decade before the Declaration of Independence and two decades before the U.S. Constitution, as was the notion that America was not only capable of standing on its own as a sovereign nation, it was preferable. In a revealing letter that Stephen Johnson wrote to his brother-in-law David Gardiner on April 12, 1763, two years before the uproar of the Stamp Act, he says, "I perceive 'tis pretty probable the Government in this North America will likely have some new modeling at home, if so the Colony of Connecticut may perhaps be more interested in it than some others—'tis a very remarkable time of health thro' the Country."

Due to its unique history, Connecticut, particularly the eastern portion of the colony, was very much interested in "some new modeling." It was self-governing, and its political and economic culture rewarded entrepreneurship and self-sufficiency. Johnson states as much in his letters, in which he makes it clear that America owes Britain nothing:

> *When our forefathers were few and poor, and incompassed with innumerable enemies, they greatly needed help and protection; yet then, there was no such concern and bustle about it: no, they were left unassisted to their own efforts, and the protection of their God. And no wonder—there was no money immediately to be got by it; but now we are numerous, and Canada and our enemies are subdued—scarce an enemy dare lift up his head in all the land—now hungry place men, and those who would be such, make a mighty bustle about our better protection—and we must be heavily taxed.*

America, Johnson notes, had always been independent and self-sufficient and ever would be so:

> *And I may add, some of the colonies have settled and defended themselves, and added a large territory and numerous subjects to the realm, and have been a great service to the mother country by their trade, and all wholly of themselves, at a vast expence of money, toil, and blood, without a farthing cost to the crown; and this they did upon the encouragement of royal charters, granted to them by the royal sovereign, under his hand and seal, expecting, and securely depending upon the privileges thereof, as an indefeasible inheritance to themselves and posterity forever. And must all be forfeit, and these privileges, securities, confidences, and expectations be all dashed in pieces and abolished at the failure of some other governments, for which they are no more accountable than the city London. Good God! Where do such sovereign measures tend, and where may they end?*

Through the writings of Lyme's Reverend Stephen Johnson, we not only experience the speeches that inspired the actions of the Sons of Liberty—we also sense the supreme confidence that these colonists, who were increasingly thinking of themselves as American citizens and not as British subjects, had in their cause and the certainty of their victory. That victory came on March 18, 1766, with the repeal of the Stamp Act. A further victory came when Thomas Fitch lost his reelection bid to New Light Jonathan Trumbull, and Patriots replaced Tories in the legislature. In Lyme, the victory of the New Lights, endorsed by the Sons of Liberty, was complete when native son Matthew Griswold IV became deputy governor of Connecticut in 1769.

By 1774, the independence-minded Trumbull-Griswold ticket would win the election in Lyme 137–1. This extraordinary dedication to the cause of liberty would characterize Lyme throughout the entire American War of Independence that was to follow.

Chapter 5

THE OLD POST ROAD

That the revolutionary words of Lyme's radical cleric Stephen Johnson printed in the *New London Gazette* struck like lightning through the colonies was in no small part due to the work of the founding father who discovered electricity, Benjamin Franklin. Long before his landmark discovery, the esteemed Dr. Franklin had been appointed deputy postmaster by the Crown, and in 1753, he went about accomplishing his first order of business: the improvement of the Post Road.

Connecting the colonies along the East Coast like a silver cord, by 1765, the Post Road was not simply an avenue of travel, it was central as a means of trade, commerce, military movements and communication. It was the spine of New England's central nervous system. The Post Road followed old Indian trails that wound their way down the coast, following the lay of the land, crossing streams at narrow fords or bending to cross at the headwaters; skirting hills and marshes, providing access to hunting grounds, open waters and neighboring villages. When the English colonists arrived, they used these established and well-worn paths for much the same purposes.

Connecticut authorities began regulating post riders as early as 1674, when correspondence was mainly carried between taverns and ordinaries. By 1691, the English Crown set about defining these paths as an official road, establishing a postal service along it to facilitate communication among the colonies and, ultimately, between America and Britain. The royal charter regulated weekly service in the summer, biweekly in the winter, along a route that ran from Baltimore, Maryland, up to Portsmouth, Maine. Passing

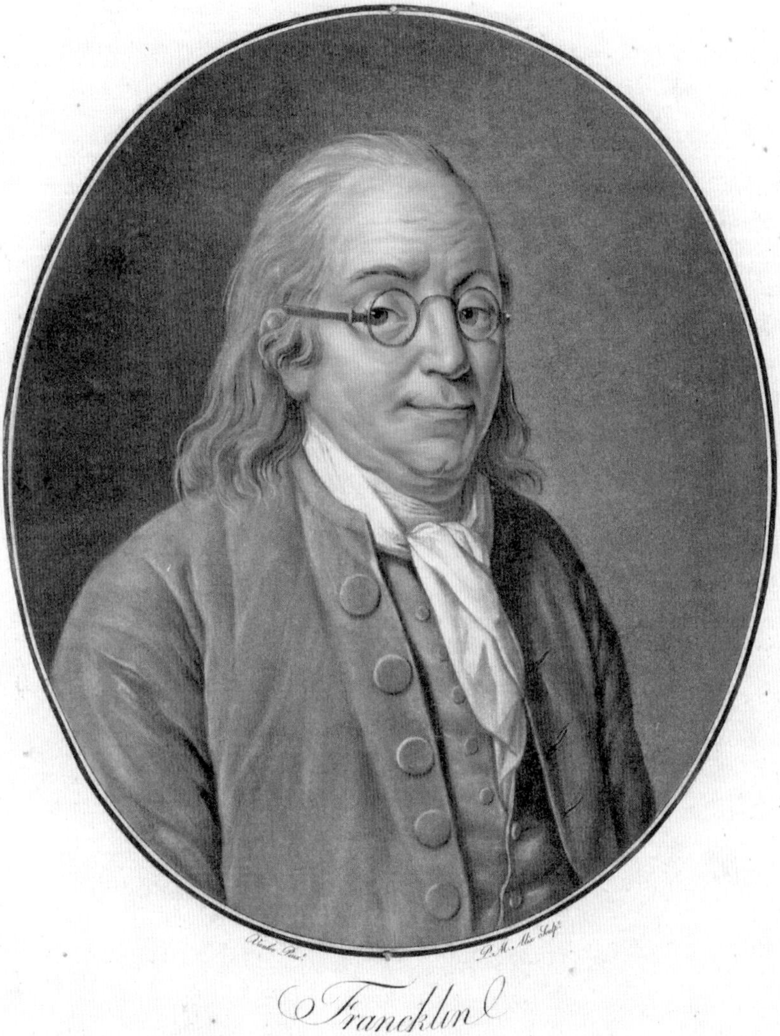

Benjamin Franklin. *New York Public Library.*

through major cities such as Philadelphia along the way, it ran along the Connecticut coast and straight through the heart of Lyme.

Situated on the eastern bank at the mouth of New England's largest river, Lyme sits halfway between the major cities of New York and Boston. As New England's population and economic activity boomed in the early eighteenth century, the need for an efficient postal system became critical to the needs of the culture in general, and business in particular. England appointed the Boston-born Philadelphia publisher, philosopher and cosmopolitan Dr. Benjamin Franklin as deputy postmaster of the American colonies.

As with any task he accepted, Franklin approached his new office with zeal and visionary innovation. He was the first postmaster to actually ride the entire route with an eye to efficiency and improvement. From this practical, and one might think pedestrian, public office, he used his position not only to make his mark as an effective administrator but also to invent a new device, the odometer, which would become a ubiquitous part of all vehicles of transportation. He would also utilize this new invention in a practical way to turn England's postal service from a debt-ridden public utility to a profit-making public service. Franklin spent ten weeks riding the Post Road through New England. He established the primary route, which strung together important towns, wayside inns, notable estates or homes of prominent families, mercantile ports and other landmarks, along with alternate routes should weather make the primary impassable. He set up regular post stops, either as dedicated post offices or designated functions of centrally located taverns or meetinghouses, and most significantly, using his newly invented odometer, he precisely measured the distances between each stop along the road and marked them with standing stones.

In a note on the corner of a map he drew in his itinerary journal in 1761, Ezra Stiles describes Franklin's invention as follows: "Benjamin Franklin by a Machine fixed to Axis of Chain Wheel in 1755 measured 14¾ miles from New London Ferry to Saybrook." Some historians dispute the date that Stiles gave for the journey, but his description of the machine Franklin invented is accurate. Having calculated the distance covered by one turn of his wagon wheel, Franklin's device clicked off each revolution of the wheel and thus was able to calculate the distance traveled. Franklin marked off the miles between points and at each mile set a stone; these would come to be known as "Franklin Milestones." Each stone marked the distance to the next postal facility, and postage rates would be fixed and regulated according to how far a letter was carried. By doing so, Franklin was able to make the postal service a profitable enterprise for the English Crown. In addition, deliveries could be made to stops along the way and charged appropriately, thus opening the miles between stations as viable locales of commerce. This innovation would aid commerce along the road, along with communication between stations, and spark an active connection that would help create a new nation.

In Lyme, Franklin set stones at one-mile intervals marking the distance to New London. One of these stones stands to this day. It is located only a few yards from the front door of Reverend Stephen Johnson's old homestead.

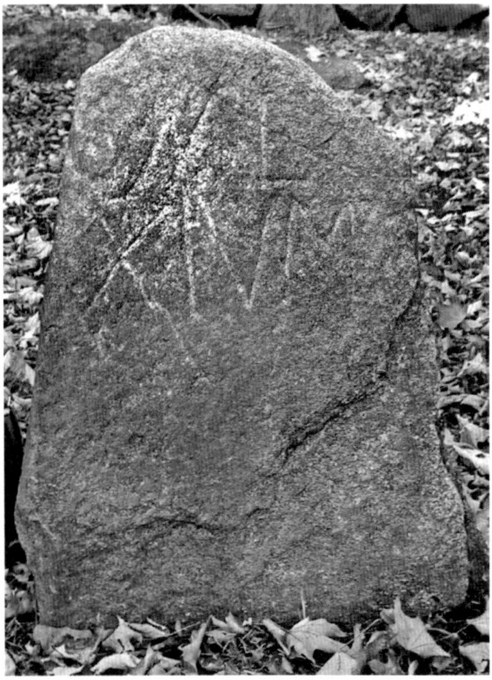

Franklin Milestone, Old Lyme. *Michaelle Pearson photo.*

A sharp-eyed traveler on Johnnycake Hill Road can still spot the granite marker that simply reads "NL XIV M": New London, fourteen miles.

Franklin himself, naturally, did not carve the stones, dig the earth or set them in place. There were professional stone carvers and setters for that task. Franklin traveled in a carriage with an odometer clicking off the distance. At the mile mark, Franklin would exit the carriage and identify the spot where a stone should be set. Following in a separate conveyance would be a carver and digger who would set the stone in the place Franklin marked. It would have been similar to how a modern-day surveying team might calculate a property line and roughly mark it with a wooden stake, which would stand until another team comes to drive an iron pin or set a merestone to bind the property.

The route that Franklin chose for the Post Road followed the old Indian trail called the Nehantic, or Shore Path. It passed the old John Winthrop farm overlooking Niantic Bay and came to the Rope Ferry at the Niantic River, under what is now the Route 156 bridge between Waterford and East Lyme. The landmark known as the Rope Ferry was so named by the means of crossing the Niantic River at this narrow, but turbulent, channel connecting the upper harbor with the lower Niantic Bay. A ferry was tethered to draft horses situated on the opposing shores. One team of horses on the western shore would pull the ferryboat toward its side, and the team of horses on the eastern shore would pull the ferryboat back.

Franklin's Post Road crossed the Rope Ferry and headed west through the tribal lands of the Nehantics, now called Niantic, marked on an Ezra Stiles map from 1768 as "wigwams along the shore." Proceeding along what is today's West Main Street, the road passed notable sites in Lyme history such as the Thomas Lee House; Bride Brook, site of Winthrop legend and New London–Lyme border dispute; and the Andrew Griswold homestead. The dispute between New London and Lyme was settled in Lyme's favor due to the pugilistic prowess of Matthew Griswold II, also known as "the Champion," son of the founder Matthew Griswold. The Post Road passed in front of the home of another Griswold descendant, Andrew Griswold, a veteran of the American Revolution. His house stood until the twentieth century, when it was torn down and replaced by a roadside motel. A milestone with Griswold's name and the distance to New London inscribed still stands in front of the Rocky Neck motel today, though it has sustained significant damage in recent years from cars, snowplows and lawn equipment.

The Post Road crossed into today's Old Lyme at the Four Mile River, near the hills overlooking the Long Island Sound that were known as Little Boston or the Well Sweep, just across from Maple Waite, where Franklin famously discovered a freshwater well. Where Route 156 crosses into Old Lyme, it becomes Shore Road. Franklin's old Post Road followed today's Shore Road until the fork with Mile Creek Road. Franklin followed Mile Creek Road through the central part of town, a fairly well-settled area that includes some of this nation's oldest surviving homesteads. At the western end of Mile Creek Road, nearly where it again merges with Shore Road, rather than following the old path that skirts the hill, Franklin's route ascended Johnnycake Hill along what is now called Ben Franklin Road.

Perhaps the best preserved portion of the Post Road as it would have appeared in Franklin's day is a dirt section of the route that begins at the end of Ben Franklin Road and joins Johnnycake Hill Road half a mile to the west. In 2006, the Town of Old Lyme relinquished its ownership of this portion of the road to private interests, and access has been limited. Only time will tell if the vague easement language of the transfer will be respected, allowing future historians free access to this site, or if the road will be forever extinguished and the town's historical legacy lost.

At Johnnycake Hill, the Post Road passed the old meetinghouse and the burying ground where many veterans of the American Revolution were laid in their final rest. Near the bottom of the hill, the road passed directly in front of Stephen Johnson's door, at the aforementioned milestone. It then joined what is today's McCurdy Road, crossing the Duck River and passing its namesake cemetery, where some of the oldest surviving headstones in America are to be found, as well as some of the best-preserved examples of the artistry of colonial stone carvers.

Just beyond the Duck River, the old Post Road curves between John McCurdy's house, still standing, and the site of the former Parsons Tavern, now known as the Ludington mansion, or Rooster Hall, across the street. Rounding the corner, it then followed Ferry Road to the Connecticut River and the ferry crossing to Saybrook.

By 1765, the path of the Post Road knit together an operative landscape of tradition, transportation and commerce and a speculative landscape of culture, communication and, increasingly, rebellion. As the cost for the creation and upkeep of roads was borne by towns, with no help from either state or Crown, and upkeep was often done by abutting property owners on a volunteer basis, the condition of the Post Road varied from town to town. In Lyme, thrift was paramount, so the road was maintained to a standard that suited local needs and took little heed of the comforts of strangers. As such, Lyme's stretch was notoriously awful, as attested by Sarah Kemble Knight in her 1704 journal. In a detailed document from 1774, Hugh Finlay, a surveyor for the Crown, called the stretch of the Post Road between Saybrook and Newport, Rhode Island, "the most difficult and dangerous as any in America."

Between September 13, 1773, and June 26, 1774, Hugh Finlay surveyed the entire length of the Post Road from Savannah, Georgia, to Casco Bay, Maine, and recorded his findings in a journal report. His experiences along the Connecticut coast are expressed in alternating tones of admiration and consternation. It is from Finlay that we learn the name of John Herd, a resident of Stamford, who was the post rider between New York and Saybrook for forty years. His counterpart who carried the mail from Saybrook and through Lyme to Newport was named Benjamin Mumford, and the tale of the two riders is illuminating. Mumford's task was unenviable. His ride was sixty miles and included five ferry crossings. He was to meet his counterpart John Herd at Saybrook at eleven o'clock on a Thursday morning, then cross the Connecticut River to Lyme and ride to the Rope Ferry, where, after crossing the Niantic River, he would spend the night. Early the next morning, he'd set out for Newport, arriving late Friday afternoon. The next Wednesday he would leave Newport in the morning and arrive at New London at six o'clock in the evening. He would then ride the additional five miles to the Rope Ferry at Lyme, where he would sleep. Upon awakening Thursday morning, he would ride the final thirteen miles to Saybrook, arriving at eleven o'clock to meet Herd, and make the return trip to Newport.

Mumford's extraordinary efforts as post rider ensured that if, for example, Ezra Stiles in Newport posted a letter to his friend Stephen Johnson in Lyme on Wednesday morning, it would arrive on Johnson's doorstep the very next day. Similarly, a newspaper published in New London on Wednesday night could arrive in either Boston or New York Friday morning. Given the limits of travel at that time, the speed and efficiency of communication along the Post Road was remarkable even by today's standards.

While communication between Newport and Lyme was fast and predictable, the leg from Saybrook to New York City was no less remarkable, if a bit more idiosyncratic. John Herd was a true Yankee of his day. Doing the rounds between Saybrook and New York reliably until well past his seventieth birthday, Herd was expert at providing necessary "additional services" to residents along the Post Road, which not only aided commerce and communication along the Connecticut coast but also padded the post rider's pocket with a bit of spare change earned via these concierge-like considerations.

Why waste a trip between Guilford and New Haven carrying only the king's post, when one could, for example, also drive a farmer's oxen, buy and sell horses and carry a merchant's wares along the way, for only a small token of consideration for his efforts? Such extra services, which often made the delivery of the mail less than predictable, met with the disapproval of royal surveyor Finlay, who raised an eyebrow at such profiteering in the course of His Majesty's service. It also drove Herd's counterpart, Mumford, who had to wait for him in Saybrook, completely crazy.

Finlay's and Mumford's complaints about Herd gained no traction, as Herd was a well loved and most useful servant along the Post Road. If he took a few extra coppers for his troubles, who could argue, as all benefited from the arrangement. Mumford, with a shorter but much more treacherous journey, could hardly afford to engage in such shenanigans along his way. If he could make his regular postal stops regardless of the vicissitudes of nature and the health of his horse without losing his shirt, he considered himself lucky.

Mumford's salary was fifty-five pounds per annum, most of which was used up by horses lost along the notoriously bad road, an expense he had to cover from his own pocket. He applied for relief from royal authorities, for a raise, for compensation for his horses or for a shortening of his route. His hopes of meeting Herd at New London rather than Saybrook were denied by the authorities, as were his other requests for relief. Perhaps posterity will provide Mumford's reward, as today's readers may applaud his efforts to expediently carry the mercurial and incendiary correspondence of commerce and revolution between Newport and Lyme.

Chapter 6
LYME'S SONS OF LIBERTY

Therefore, as a Son of Liberty, I expect to be judged by my peers and neighbors in this affair.
—John McCurdy, Lyme, July 12, 1770

John McCurdy was a staunch Patriot and one of the wealthiest merchants in Connecticut. He lived on the Post Road in Lyme, just around the bend from Reverend Stephen Johnson, and was not only a successful merchant but also a man of letters who possessed one of the most extensive personal libraries in the region. Though he was not a lawyer or clergyman, his collection included a number of legal and theological texts, as well as history, philosophy and literature, and was considered one of the most impressive in the colony. This placed McCurdy in good company with Lyme's other leading lights, many of whom were Yale or Harvard men, who, as evidenced in town records, left impressive libraries to their progeny. But McCurdy, like Matthew Griswold, was an autodidact who could not only hold his own in an intellectual conversation but could also lead that conversation and educate others. Johnson, whose own collection held Locke and Montesquieu, often spent evenings in McCurdy's library, studying volumes of Enlightenment philosophy, classical literature and theology. They engaged in lively conversation on matters political and spiritual and became close friends. It was McCurdy who encouraged Johnson's incendiary articles on the Stamp Act and carried those articles to Timothy Green in New London for publication in the *Gazette*, kindling the spark that started a revolution. McCurdy was also the agent who secreted documents from Sons of Liberty

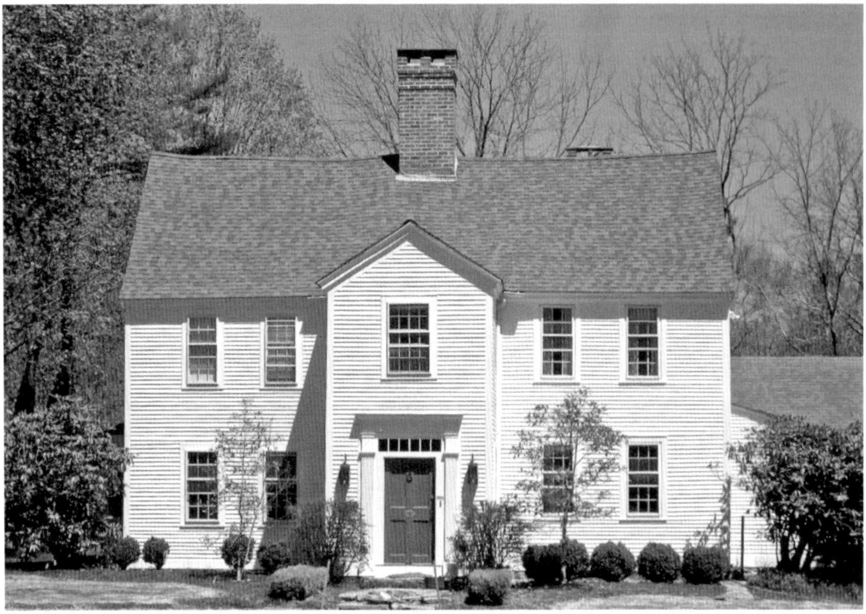

Peck Tavern, Old Lyme, 2016. *Michaelle Pearson photo.*

in New York City, then a Tory stronghold, to Patriot-controlled New London for publication.

John McCurdy was well connected in New York City, as he lived there after emigrating from Ireland in 1745. He quickly established himself as a merchant and by 1753 had moved to Lyme, where he opened a store in the Peck Tavern, bought the Amos Tinker house on Lyme Street and commanded a fleet of merchant vessels that plied the West Indies and Ireland trades. His specialties included bringing Connecticut mill horses to St. Kitts for use in the cane fields in exchange for molasses and rum and a more curious trade of carrying flaxseed to Ireland in exchange for finished goods. While carrying flaxseed to Ireland may have seemed like "carrying coals to Newcastle," flax from eastern Connecticut was known to be the finest in the world, and McCurdy became its chief purveyor. He kept a firm hand in his affairs and often personally undertook the journey to St. Kitts or Dublin aboard one of his ships so he could negotiate terms and maintain personal oversight.

Direct, devout in his beliefs and dedicated to his business, McCurdy had friends and business associates in power centers of the British Empire who were becoming restless and straining under the yoke of ministerial rule from London. A series of royal decrees and ministerial acts in the mid-eighteenth

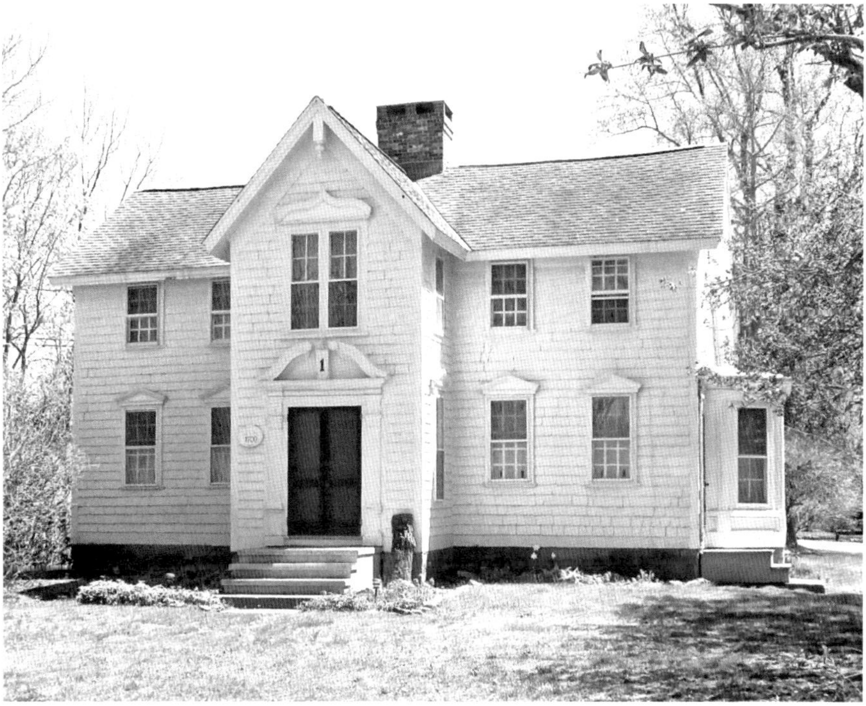

John McCurdy House, Old Lyme, 2016. *Michaelle Pearson photo.*

century sought to tighten political control over Ireland, dominate the West Indies trade and raise revenue from the American colonies. In each case, McCurdy's personal interests were at stake.

The Sugar Act, passed in 1764, sought to ban all direct trade between the American colonies and French, Spanish and Dutch islands in the West Indies, funneling all American trade through English-controlled ports and collecting duties on molasses imported to America from the West Indies. Along the Connecticut coast, the Sugar Act was often circumvented or ignored, and if the matter was pressed, the customary practice of bribing the official charged with enforcement usually did the trick. Commercial maritime interests in Connecticut had long been accustomed to handling their own affairs and determining and regulating their own business practices, and it would take more than a few agents from London to change their ways. It was well known that the flaxseed barrels bound for Dublin were oftentimes "accidentally" filled with molasses, and customs officials generally looked the other way.

It was not surprising that the merchant vessels of ports such as Lyme and New London would later be easily pressed into service as privateers in the cause of American freedom and, as such, provide the new nation with an instant navy to challenge the world's mightiest. Not coincidentally, many of John McCurdy's own ships became privateers carrying letters of marque permitting them to seize British vessels. Perhaps it was also no coincidence that, in 1765, the fiercest resistance to the Stamp Act outside of New England occurred on the island of St. Kitts, where liberty poles were erected, stampmen were hanged in effigy and violent riots marked the resistance. That McCurdy was prominent in the St. Kitts trade and known personally to the islanders may have been an influential factor in the fierce nature of the opposition on St. Kitts.

The image of ragtag soldiers, farmers and journeymen led by heroic "great men" such as Washington, loyally fighting together for America's freedom from Britain, is one well founded in fact, but it is not a complete picture. Just as striking and important a portrait is of that of men such as John McCurdy or his friend New London publisher Timothy Green: men of prominence, influence and wealth who were willing to put their own treasure and often their very lives at risk for the cause of independence. Their positions owed little or nothing to Britain. In fact, their influence and wealth did not depend on British patronage—it was often in spite of it. Grounded in successful enterprises, fueled by Enlightenment philosophy and encouraged by a local culture founded over one hundred years earlier on the principles of economic and political self-determination, these men had both the confidence and means to resist British rule.

Timothy Green, in particular, prominently fixed his name upon the cause of revolution, practically taunting British authorities to arrest him or seize his operations. The Green family name is synonymous with publishing in colonial New England, especially in Boston, Hartford, New Haven and New London. Samuel Green of Cambridge, Massachusetts, was the successor of Stephen Daye, the first printer in North America. The first printing press in the Americas, known as the "Daye Press" or "Dresden Press," was a seventeenth-century press imported from Germany. The Daye Press was purchased by Samuel Green and later brought to New London by his son Timothy Green in 1713. It was on this press that the second Timothy Green, son of the first, began a newspaper called the *New London Summary* in 1758. Continuing the family tradition, Timothy Green III, who was actually the son of Timothy Green II's brother Samuel, transformed the *New London Summary* into a broadsheet called the *New London Gazette*.

When John McCurdy had in his possession writings from New York's Sons of Liberty or from Reverend Stephen Johnson protesting British rule

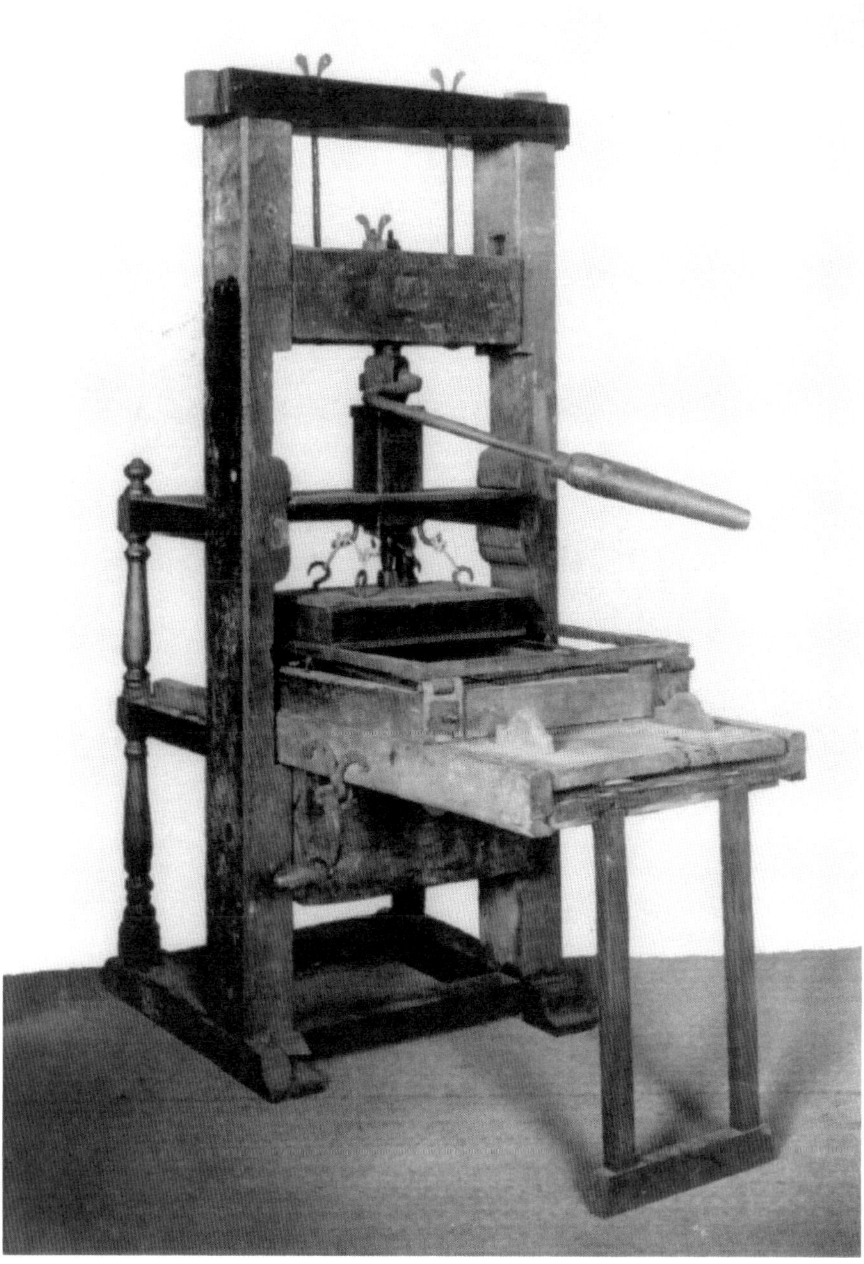

The Daye Press/Dresden Press, 1639, was the first press in the American colonies. Timothy Green of New London put it to good use, printing the *Connecticut Gazette* and secret documents smuggled from New York's Sons of Liberty by Lyme's John McCurdy. *Library of Congress, Prints and Photographs Division.*

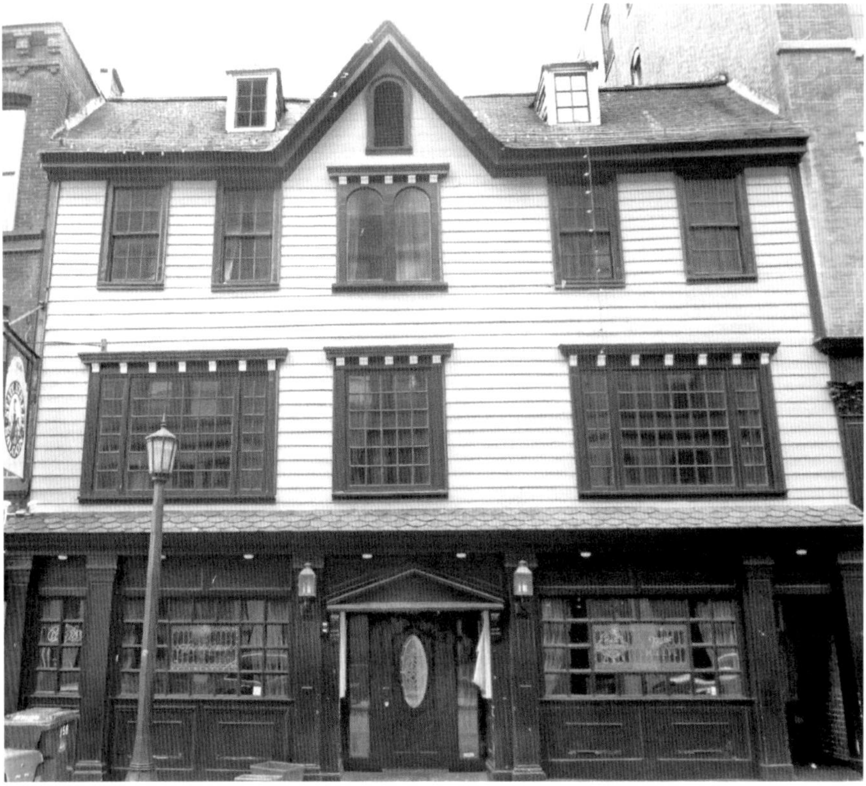

Timothy Green's publishing house, New London, 2016. *Jim Lampos photo.*

and advocating rebellion, he brought them to Timothy Green III in New London. In Green, he found not only a friend and kindred spirit but also a publisher from a family who was the first name in New England's history of letters, who would willingly print those incendiary tracts on the first press operating in North America. Thus, the most radical tradition of New England thought found its ultimate expression within the deepest roots of its publishing concerns and was immortalized on its original press.

To hold an original copy of the *New London Gazette* in hand today and feel the sturdy, cloth-like rag paper still fresh and vibrant after 250 years, with Johnson's letters impressed upon it—letters that were carried to publisher Timothy Green by John McCurdy—is to experience the life force of American history directly through the hand of these Patriots.

Issue No. 105 of the *New London Gazette*, dated November 15, 1765, replaced its usual masthead depicting England's lion and Scotland's unicorn with a simple legend: "Liberty and Property, and NO STAMPS." This was an act of defiance by Green and the writers he published against the Crown. In the face of strong resistance from the colonies, Britain stood down, and the Stamp Act was repealed on March 18, 1766. However, victory in the battle against the Stamp Act proved to be merely the opening act of a full war between America and Britain. For a short time, it appeared that cooler heads on both sides of the Atlantic might prevail. Furtive discussions among American-sympathizing ministers who thought British actions too heavy-handed and American diplomats and officeholders who thought their own countrymen unreasonable and hotheaded began in earnest in an attempt to breach the divide between the mother country and its errant child and come to a mutually agreed upon resolution, whereby the Crown could raise necessary revenues and the colonists could continue unfettered in their enterprising ways. On the American side, there was the philosophe and cosmopolitan Franklin, and on the British, statesman William Pitt. When push came to shove, both men had to jump.

It took just one year for Britain to readjust its strategy and try a new tactic for raising revenue. The Townshend Acts, named after British minister Charles Townshend and passed in 1767, levied a tax on glass, lead, tea, paint and paper imported into the American colonies. The tax would be collected at the port of entry, and the newly formed board of customs collectors would be charged with enforcement. Americans immediately responded by banning all importation of goods from Britain and setting up their own committees of inspection to ensure that merchants were not trading with the government they once called the mother country. Confident in their ability to not only resist British authority but also to cut off all economic ties and still prosper, the colonists began a process that would build a national economy and culture completely self-reliant and independent from Britain in all but the letter of the law. Resistance to British goods, especially at the expense of comfort and fashion, was seen as the mark of a Patriot.

It was in this atmosphere of economic resistance that the patriotism of John McCurdy came into question. In July 1770, the Committee of Inspection of New York accused John McCurdy, along with Lyme's Captain Elisha Merrow and New York merchant George Thomson, of violating the nonimportation agreement by importing into New York, in Merrow's words, "a parcel of checks, pins, ribands, knee-garters, tammies, etc., and for ignominously fleeing from justice." Merrow protested that he had assurances and paperwork from McCurdy that the articles in question had been obtained before the ban on imports, and rather than fleeing from justice, he was running for his life when he left New York City. Merrow's letter to the

New London Gazette dated July 12, 1770, reads: "[W]hen I got to York, there was nothing but fire and sword, burning goods, knocking one another in the head, some for importation, others against it." He then met with New York's Committee of Inspection and offered proof of his innocence:

> *Some of the committee advised me privately to take care of myself and vessel—Before I had time to get to her, sundry gentlemen in the street told me to make the best of my way, for there was information gone to the custom house against me, and everyone that could get a hand to my vessel helped me out of the dock. Now was this ignominiously fleeing from justice? No, but rather from ravening wolves, from destruction and flames with which I was threatened.*

McCurdy defended himself in two letters: one to the *Gazette* and one to the Merchant's Committee in New London, both dated July 12. The Merchant's Committee letter was also reprinted in the *Gazette* on July 27. In the first letter, McCurdy asserts that he had "neither directly nor indirectly; nor never have had one article of goods in my shop, that I imported, either from Great Britain or Rhode Island, since the non-importation took place." He further notes, "As to the committee of New York, many of them are gentlemen, and well known to me to be such, and from whom I have received many favors; others of them I am unacquainted with."

His second letter to the Merchant's Committee of New London is more detailed, and in it he states, "I never have had one shilling worth of goods in my shop that I imported from Great Britain or Rhode Island, since the non-importation took place. And if I had it in my power, no man else on the continent should import till all the acts were repealed that we complain of."

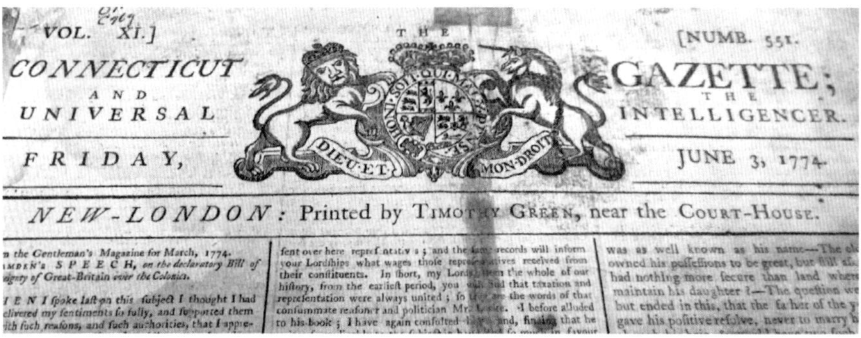

Connecticut Gazette masthead with the Royal Seal of Great Britain, 1774. *New London County Historical Society*.

To this clear statement of political loyalty, McCurdy added, "It sits ill on my stomach to be impeached with those things that are contrary to my well-known principles, by all those that are acquainted with me. Therefore, as a Son of Liberty, I expect to be judged by my peers and neighbors in this affair."

Lyme's Sons of Liberty, formed to protest the Stamp Act, did not disband after the act's repeal, but rather continued to prosper and strengthen as an active enforcement arm of American patriotic initiatives. While membership rolls were rarely made public, McCurdy publicly counted himself among their ranks, and numerous sources concur that Matthew Griswold and Stephen Johnson were also among their number. The actions of all three men clearly demonstrated the zeal and principles of the Sons of Liberty, and it would be passing strange if they were not members in fact.

The Sons of Liberty would take center stage in 1774 through a series of political actions in response to Britain's Intolerable Acts that inevitably signaled a coming war. Perhaps the most famous Son of Liberty was Boston's Samuel Adams. In a prescient letter to Adams from Lyme's Samuel Holden Parsons dated March 3, 1773, Parsons writes, "The idea of unalienable allegiance to any prince or state is an idea to me inadmissible and I can't see but that our ancestors when they first landed in America were as independent on the Crown or King of Great Britain as if they had never been his subjects."

The events of the next three years would bring Samuel Holden Parsons and his father, Reverend Jonathan Parsons, along with Jonathan's successor to Lyme's Congregational ministry, Reverend Stephen Johnson, together in the city of Boston, in the midst of a battle that would pit colony against empire and citizen against sovereign. The modern world, based on the ideas of the Enlightenment, was about to be born, and Lyme had no small part in its conception.

Chapter 7

LYME HOSTS A TEA PARTY

LYME March 17, 1774.

Yesterday, one William Lamson of Martha's Vineyard came to this town with a bag of tea (about 100 wt) on horseback which he was peddling about the country. It appeared that he was about business which (he supposed) would render him obnoxious to the people which gave reason to suspect that he had some of the detestable tea lately landed at Cape Cod; and upon examination it appeared to the satisfaction of all present to be part of that very tea; (though he declared that he purchased it of two gentlemen in Newport, one of them 'tis said is custom house officer and other Captain of the fort) whereupon a number of the Sons of Liberty assembled in the evening, kindled a fire and committed its contents to the flames where it was all consumed and the ashes buried on the spot, in testimony of their utter abhorrence of all tea subject to a duty for the purpose of raising a revenue in America. A laudable example for our brethren in Connecticut.

—Connecticut Courant, *March 22, 1774*

Thus read the account of Lyme's tea party, as it appeared in newspapers throughout the colonies in the spring of 1774. Though not as famous as the oft-told tale of Boston's tea party, Lyme's affair was a celebrated event in the colonies, telling as to the feelings of the public toward the British Acts, and stood as admonition to Tories and traitors of the fate they could meet at the hands of Lyme's Sons of Liberty.

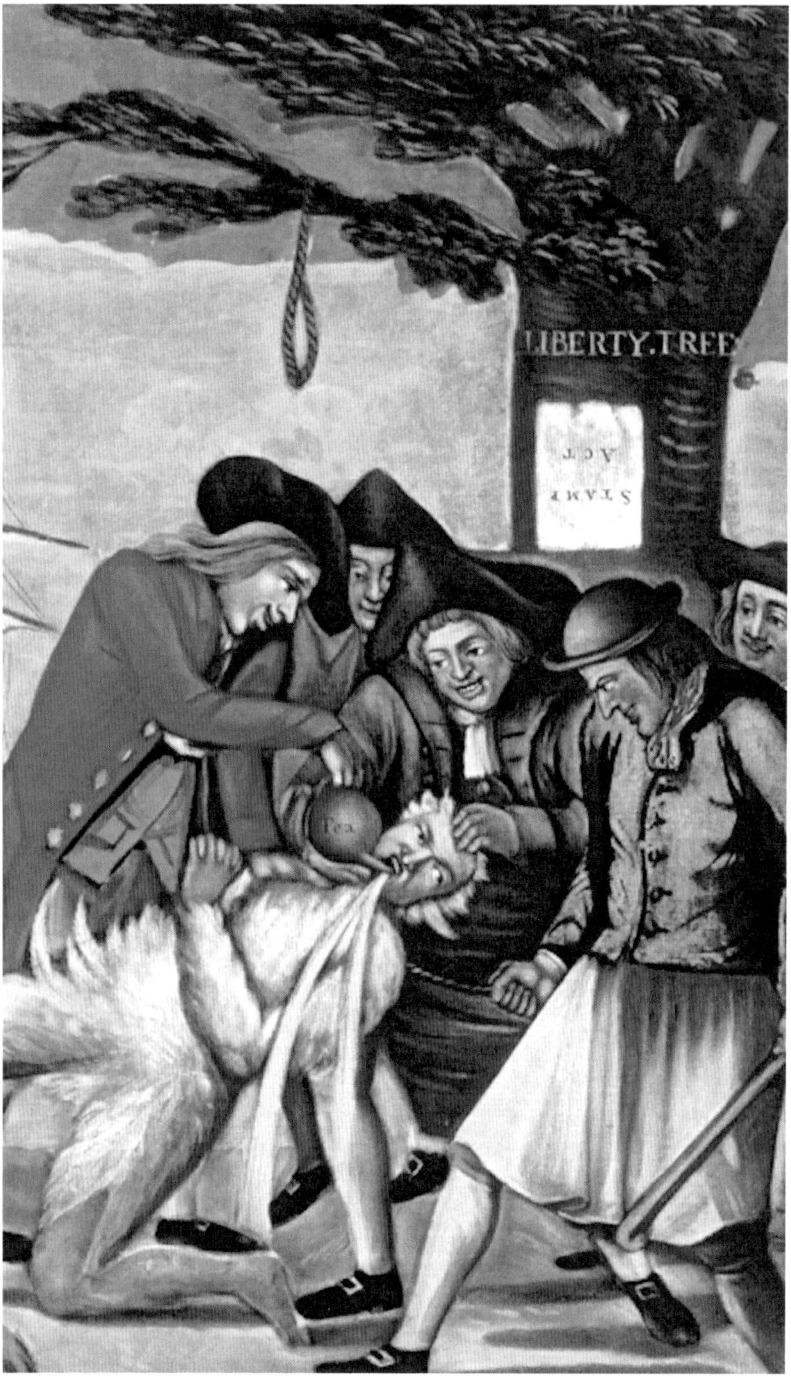

Paying the Excise Man, detail, 1774. *Library of Congress.*

The errant peddler was seized on the town green along the Post Road and his tea set ablaze in the middle of the street, at a spot near today's Congregational church. The ultimate fate of peddler Lamson is not reported, but this account is fairly mild compared to the treatment Connecticut Tories would receive at the hands of Patriots through the end of the decade.

The actions of Parliament at this time were seen as being either too clever by half or simply clueless. Perhaps no act exhibited each of those qualities in greater abundance than the Tea Act of 1773. Seen by the king's ministers as a sly way of "cutting taxes" for Americans while raising revenues for Britain, with the added bonus of simultaneously propping up the failing East India Company, the Tea Act authorized the East India Company to ship tea directly into American ports and regulate that trade. In the past, East India tea had to land in Britain and, subject to tax, was purchased by American middlemen who imported it to the colonies. By authorizing the East India Company to deal directly with America, the cost to the American consumer would be cut, and thus, it was assumed, consumption would increase. Revenues from America to the British treasury would be enhanced due to the spike in consumption, but though they would be paying more tax, the British thought the colonists would be grateful, as the overall cost of tea would be lower. In the eyes of Britain's ministers, it should have been a win-win. Instead, it was met with derision. British tea was dumped in Boston's harbor, burned at Lyme's town green and generally scorned by a population who learned to suddenly embrace coffee and native herbs as the patriotic elixirs of choice.

In retaliation for the destruction of the tea at Boston, Britain cracked down with a series of "Coercive Acts" designed to restore order and discipline to the unruly colonies. On March 25, 1774, Britain authorized the closure of the port of Boston to all shipping, effective June 1 and continuing indefinitely until such time as the East India Company was compensated for damages by the citizens of Massachusetts. In May, when no reparations were forthcoming, Britain passed the Massachusetts Government Act, which revoked that colony's charter and placed it under direct control of the Crown.

That same month, the British Parliament passed the Administration of Justice Act, known to Americans as "The Murder Act," which permitted any employee of the British government, whether they be royal official, agent or a soldier accused of a crime in America, to be removed to London for trial. Americans saw this as a device that would allow Brits to get away with any crime they wished.

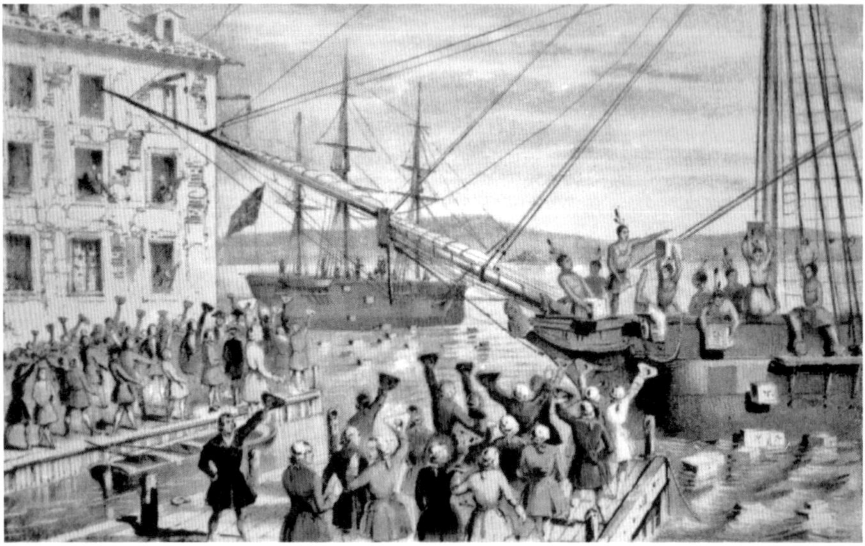

Destruction of the Tea at Boston Harbor, Currier & Ives. *Library of Congress, Prints and Photographs Division.*

In June, the Quartering Act was amended, renewing the rarely enforced act of the same name passed in 1765 and giving the royally appointed governor authority to seize buildings for the quartering of British soldiers. Together, these acts were termed the "Intolerable Acts" by Americans. Rather than cowing the population into subservience or obedience, they galvanized colonists already intellectually committed to independence and prepared them to prove that commitment in blood.

Meetings were held in towns throughout Connecticut in June 1774 to determine "proper measures to be pursued in the present alarming State of America" and set up Committees of Correspondence, whereby actions could be communicated and coordinated among various towns and colonies.

In Lyme, the meeting was held on June 20, and attendees voted to appoint John McCurdy; Eleazer Mather, Esq.; John Lay; William Noyes, Esq.; and Samuel Mather to the Committee of Correspondence and directed that Boston's committee be informed of the vote. Lyme's citizens again gathered at town meeting on September 13 to authorize the building of a powder house and order the doubling of militia exercises. For a population that was ostensibly averse to taxes, they also voted at that meeting to raise funds for the defense of Boston and appointed Samuel Selden, Esq.; Samuel Ely, Esq.; Captain Elisha Marvin; Richard Wait; Elijah Smith; Captain Jonathan

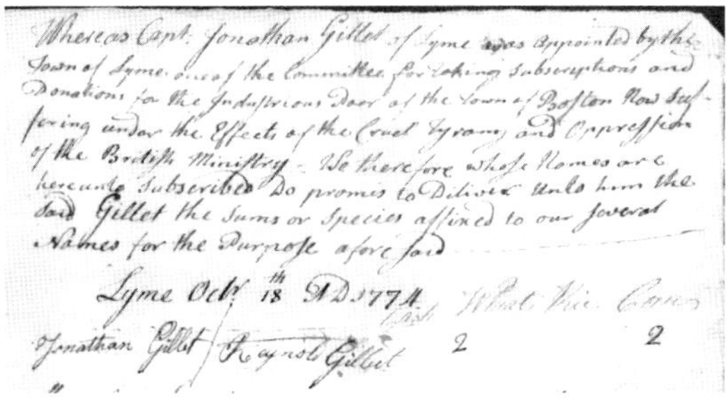

Whereas Capt. Jonathan Gillet of Lyme was Appointed by the Town of Lyme one of the Committee for taking Subscriptions and Donations for the Industrious Poor of the Town of Boston Now Suffering under the Effects of the Cruel Tyranny and Oppression of the British Ministry. We therefore whose Names are hereunto Subscribed Do promise to Deliver unto him the said Gillet the Sums or Species affixed to our several Names for the Purpose aforesaid

Lyme Octr 18th AD 1774

Jonathan Gillet | Reynold Gillet 2 2

Promissory note to Captain Jonathan Gillet for donations raised to aid "the Industrious Poor of the Town of Boston, now suffering under the Effects of the Cruel Tyranny and Oppression of the British Ministry," 1774. *Lyme Historical Society Archives, Florence Griswold Museum.*

Gillet; Benjamin Lee, Esq.; and John McCurdy to conduct the fundraising and transmit the funds to the beleaguered citizens of Boston.

In October, the Connecticut General Assembly called for town selectmen to double the amount of munitions on hand and muster militias for extra training. These actions had already been agreed to by a convention of delegates from Windham and New London Counties on September 8. On all fronts, New Englanders were drawing closer together, coordinating their actions, coming to the relief of those under British oppression and placing themselves on a war footing.

By 1774, the Connecticut economy had been booming nearly unabated since its founding nearly 150 years prior, under the autonomous direction of the colonists themselves, with a steadily growing population. It was an economy that thrived on free trade and *Mare Liberum*, or liberty of the seas. Near Lyme, a 1774 ad from the *Norwich Packet* lists the items for sale at Thomas Coit's store on Norwich Harbor. These included:

> *Madeira, Lisbon and Malaga Wines, Claret, Best Jamaican Spirits, West India and New England Rum, Molasses, Brandy, Geneva, Loaf and Brown Sugar, Tea, Coffee, Chocolate, Indigo, Rice, Raisins, Ginger, Pepper, Allspice, Cinnamon, Mace, Cloves, Nutmegs, Allum, Redwood, Logwood, Madder, Copper, Powder and Shot, White and Red Lead, Spanish Brown, Nails, Brads, Glass, Long and Short Pipes; Earth Glass and "Delph" ware; Glass Bottles, and Velvet.*

John McCurdy's store in Lyme was similarly stocked with items from all over the world. But this bustling economy was now nearing collapse under a resurgence of British authoritarianism. Money became worthless, and farms were abandoned or put up for sale at bargain rates. John McCurdy closed his store at the Peck Tavern and for the next year was dedicated to collecting the debts owed him. Destiny and commerce both demanded a resolution of

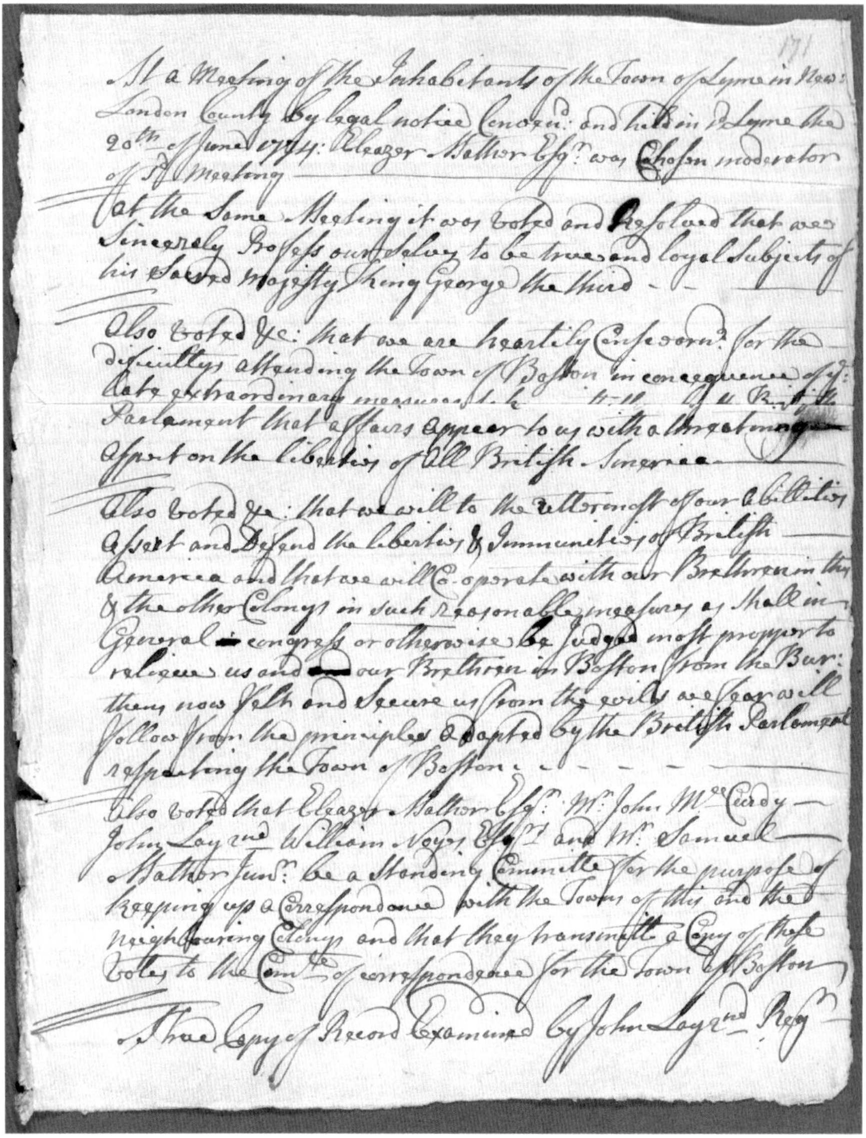

171

At a Meeting of the Inhabitants of the Town of Lyme in New London County by legal notice Convened and held in sd Lyme the 20th of June 1774: Eleazer Mather Esqr was Chosen moderator of sd Meeting

At the Same Meeting it was voted and Resolved that we Sincerely Profess our Selves to be true and loyal Subjects of his Sacred Majesty King George the third

Also voted &c: that we are heartily Concern'd for the difficultys attending the Town of Boston in consequence of ye late extraordinary measures [illegible] Brittish Parlament that affairs appear to us with a threatning aspect on the liberties of all British America

Also voted &c: that we will to the uttermost of our abilities assert and Defend the liberties & Immunities of British America and that we will Co-operate with our Brethren in this & the other Colonys in such Reasonable measures as shall in General congress or otherwise be judged most proper to relieve us and our Brethren in Boston from the Burthens now felt and Secure us from the evils we fear will follow from the principles adopted by the British Parlement respecting the Town of Boston

Also voted that Eleazer Mather Esqr Mr John McCurdy John Lay 2nd William Noyes Esqr and Mr Samuel Mather Junr be a Standing Committee for the purpose of keeping up a Correspondence with the Towns of this and the Neighbouring Colonys and that they transmitt a Copy of these votes to the Comtee of correspondence for the Town of Boston

A true Copy of Record Examined by John Lay 2nd Regr

Lyme Correspondence Committee, June 20, 1774. *New York Public Library.*

the political question, and that question is this: upon what power does the legitimacy of the government rest?

The Connecticut House of Representatives, in which Matthew Griswold and Samuel H. Parsons had both served, answered this question in no uncertain terms in May 1774, stating, "[T]he only lawful Representatives of

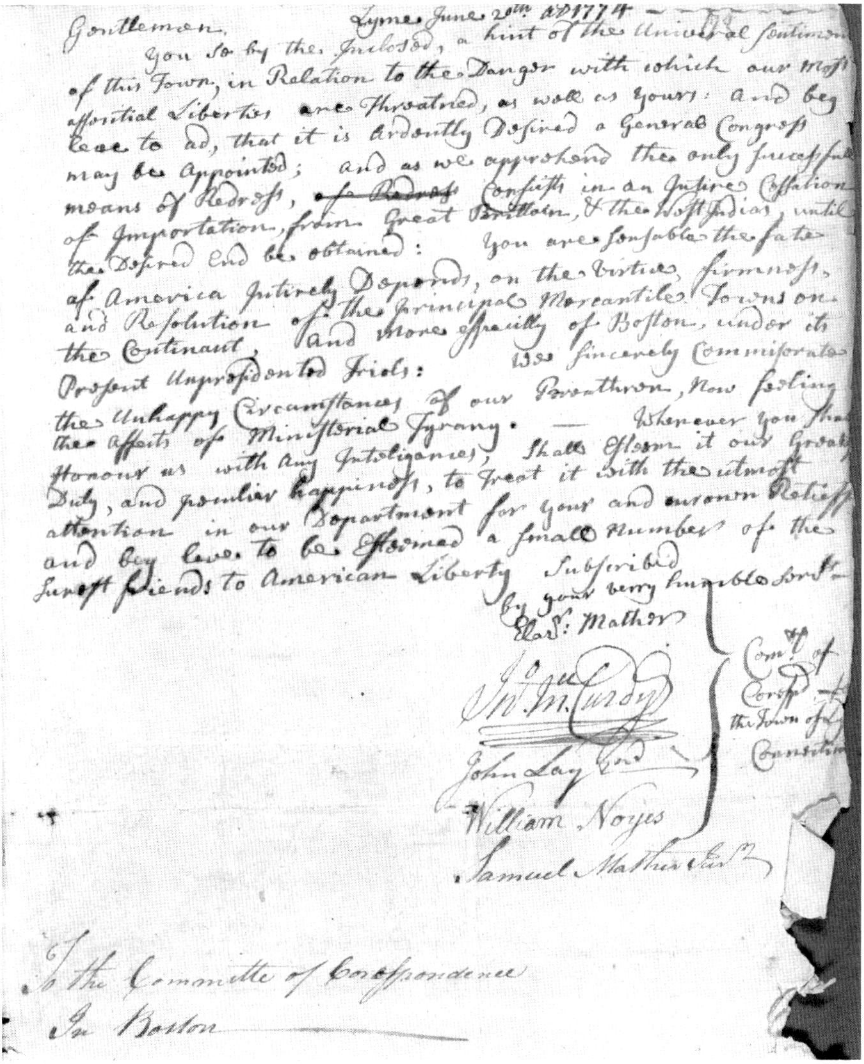

Lyme June 20th AD1774 —

Gentlemen,

You see by the Inclosed, a hint of the Universal sentiment of this Town, in Relation to the Danger with which our most essential Liberties are Threatned, as well as yours: and beg leave to ad, that it is Ardently Desired a General Congress may be Appointed; and as we apprehend the only successful means of Redress, consists in an Intire Cessation of Importation, from Great Brittain, & the West Indias, until the Desired End be obtained: You are sensable the fate of America intirely Depends, on the Virtue, firmness, and Resolution of the principal Mercantile Towns on the Continant, and more especially of Boston, under its Present Unprecedented Trials: We sincerely Commiserate the Unhappy Circumstances of our Brethren, Now feeling the effects of Ministerial Tyrany. — Whenever You shall Honour us with any Intelligences, Shall Esteem it our Great Duty, and peculiar happiness, to Treat it with the utmost attention in our Department for your and our own Relief and beg leave to be Esteemed a small number of the surest friends to American Liberty Subscribed by your very humble servt—

El[illegible] Mather

Jn. McCurdy

John Lay 2nd

William Noyes

Samuel Mather Jun.

Comt. of Corresp— the Town of [illegible] Committee

To the Committee of Correspondence

In Boston

Lyme Correspondence Committee, June 20, 1774. *New York Public Library.*

the Freemen of the Colony are the persons they elect to serve as Members of the General Assembly thereof."

From that moment on, the acts of the British Parliament were null and void in the minds of Patriots. The wisdom of British strategy was questioned within the halls of Parliament itself. The *Norwich Packet* reported on May 26, 1774, that in a rancorous debate over the Boston Port Bill, Parliamentarian George Dempster rose to remind his fellow British lawmakers that "our disorders had arisen from our attempt to tax the Americans by that odious Stamp Act" and went on to ask "what limits or line is drawn" to circumscribe the king's powers. "Had we not given an extent of power to his Majesty, to prevent the port of Boston from ever being reinstated?" The American question called up ancient divisions within the politics of Britain itself and reignited the question of the balance of power between monarch and legislature—a question that precipitated the English Civil War in the 1630s and had been revisited many times over the previous century and a half.

Reverend Stephen Johnson's prediction that the end result of Britain's authoritarian actions against the American colonies would result not in subjugation, but rather civil war in Britain, suddenly did not seem like a fanciful or idle threat. The Intolerable Acts strengthened American unity and resolve while reopening old fault lines that divided Britain itself.

American entreaties for fair treatment and representation in British Parliament, while finding sympathetic ears within Britain, only met with increasing disdain and dismissal from King George III and his ministers. When the king opened Parliament in December 1774, he condemned the "most daring spirit of resistance and disobedience to the law" and vowed "firm and steadfast resolution to withstand every attempt to weaken or impair the supreme authority of the Legislature over all the dominions of the Crown." A hard line was drawn, and the colonists could no longer comfort themselves with the hope that their merciful king would be persuaded to see the justice of their cause. Through that winter, they stopped drafting pleas and turned to building their communal stores of powder and shot and preparing their well-organized town militias for the inevitable conflict. The Connecticut Assembly voted in January 1775 to have towns muster and drill their militias weekly, standing in sharp readiness to defend their liberties. That winter was the warmest in memory. The dark days and heavy snows of the boreal season usually kept the colonists close to home, tending their livestock or going on short hunting excursions, but not venturing forth on long journeys or undertaking grand ventures. But the uneasy autumn of '74 gave way to a restless winter, unseasonable in temperature and disquieted in emotion, which did nothing to cool the ardor of the Patriots. By the early spring of 1775, the British occupying Boston and blockading the harbor had countenanced the sneers and jeers of patriotic New Englanders long enough and sought once and for all to rout these treasonous rebels. The Americans, who had been organizing, mustering and gathering courage, knew the moment was at hand. The time had arrived for Patriots to raise a standard for themselves and their posterity. The result would be in the hand of Divine Providence.

Chapter 8

Israel Bissel's Ride

Hoofbeats shook the ground as they pounded down the hill, coming to a stop just outside Reverend Stephen Johnson's house on Lyme's Post Road. Heavy knocking aroused the minister from his slumber, and when he threw open the door, there stood twenty-three-year-old minuteman Israel Bissel crying, "TO ARMS! TO ARMS! THE WAR HAS BEGUN!" The minuteman quickly thrust his dispatch into the clergyman's hand. The document, from the Massachusetts Provincial Congress's Committee of Safety in Watertown, read:

> *To all friends of American Liberty, be it known, this morning before break of day, a Brigade, consisting of about 1000 to 1200 men, landed at Phipps Farm at Cambridge and marched to Lexington, where they found a Company of our Militia in Arms, upon whom they fired without any provocation and killed 6 men and wounded 4 others—By an express from Boston we find another Brigade are now upon their March from Boston, supposed to be about 1000—The Bearer, Israel Bissel, is charged to alarm the Country quite to Connecticut, and all Persons are desired to furnish him with fresh Horses, as they may be needed—I have spoken with several who have seen the dead and wounded. —J. Palmer, one of the Committee Of S--- Y---*

This time, Johnson would not be writing another incendiary letter to the *Gazette*. Instead, he immediately raised the militia, so that within days, Lyme's men—said to be one hundred strong—marched to the defense of their Massachusetts brethren. They were joined by four thousand other Connecticut men who answered the call to arms.

British troops engaged in what they thought was a routine mission to seize a cache of rebel arms in Concord and make a show of force from the world's most formidable army—sending a message to New England's Patriots that the time had come to toe the line—were instead instantly swarmed and outnumbered by a surprisingly disciplined and armed band of New England citizens. This American army comprised men from all walks of life: doctors, ministers, farmers, journeymen, lawyers, tradesmen and laborers, who seemingly appeared from nowhere to answer the shots fired in Lexington and, repelling the incursion, harassed the British brigade along every step of their ignoble retreat back to Boston.

The war against Britain had begun. Reverend Stephen Johnson, from whose pen came the earliest and most eloquent expressions of justification for the cause of American independence, would himself march to Boston as a member of Samuel Holden Parsons's Sixth Regiment, offering to seal his revolutionary words in blood, whether it be his enemy's or his own.

Israel Bissel set out from Watertown, Massachusetts, at 10:00 a.m. on Wednesday, April 19, to spread the news of the alarm from Lexington through southern New England and into New York. Though not as famous as the most celebrated rider of the Lexington alarm, Paul Revere, whose exploits were immortalized by the great bard Longfellow, Bissel's ride was just as heroic and even more remarkable than Revere's. Leaving Watertown, Bissel arrived at Worcester by the evening, whereupon his horse dropped dead in its tracks. With a fresh horse, he rode hard to Brooklyn, Connecticut, arriving at 11:00 a.m. on Thursday. There he met Israel Putnam, the fifty-seven-year-old veteran of the French and Indian War, New Light member of the general assembly, Freemason and ardent Son of Liberty. Putnam was out plowing his field but, on hearing Bissel's news, dropped his plow, took up arms and rode to Cambridge to join the American resistance. Over the next few years, Putnam would become one of the most celebrated generals in the American War of Independence.

Not wasting time, Bissel continued his ride. By 4:00 p.m., he had arrived at Christopher Leffingwell's in Norwich, and by 7:00 p.m. he made it to New London and met with Lyme's Colonel Samuel Holden Parsons, who was serving there as regiment commander and a member of the Committee of Correspondence. Parsons signed off on Bissel's alarm and sent him on his way. Following the Post Road, the minuteman crossed the Rope Ferry at Niantic and arrived in Lyme, at Reverend Johnson's door, at 1:00 a.m.

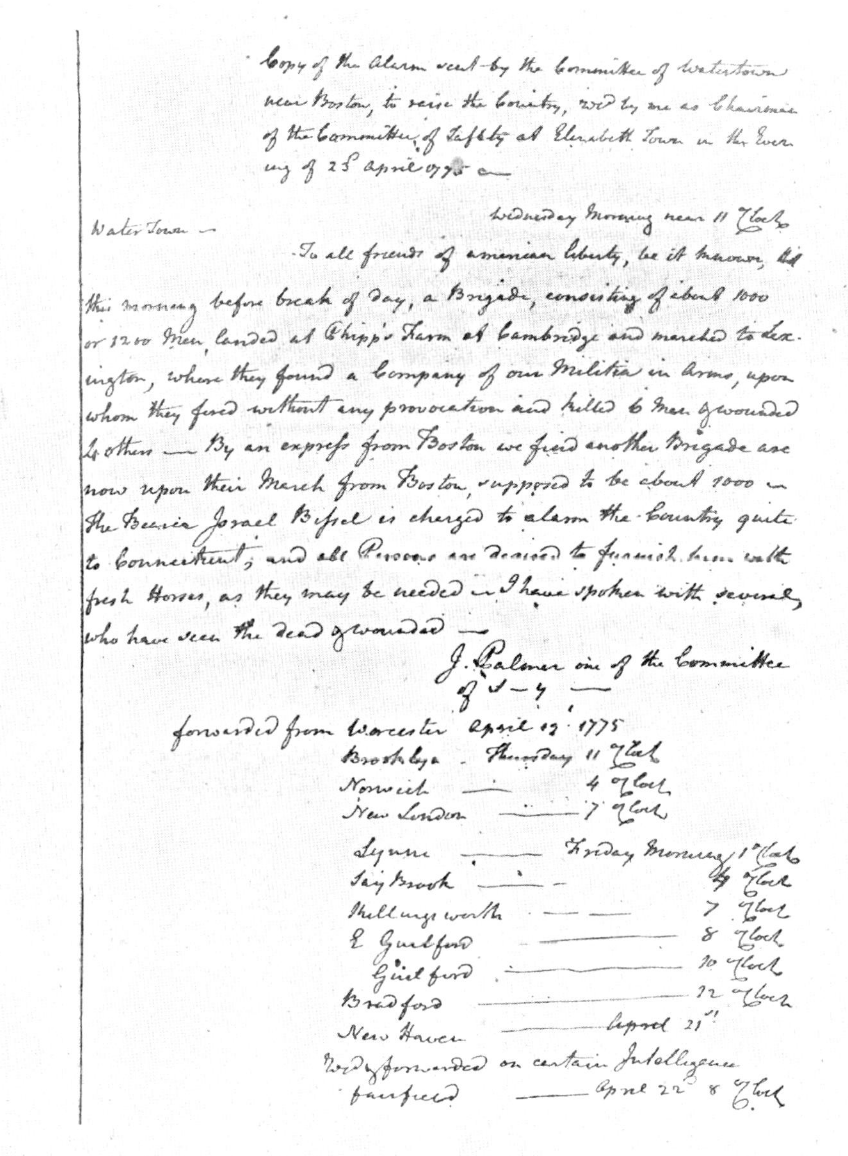

Copy of the Alarm sent by the Committee of Watertown near Boston, to raise the Country, rec'd by me as Chairman of the Committee of Safety at Elizabeth Town in the Evening of 25 April 1775 —

Water Town — Wednesday Morning near 11 o'Clock

To all friends of american liberty, be it known, that this morning before break of day, a Brigade, consisting of about 1000 or 1200 Men, landed at Phipp's Farm at Cambridge and marched to Lexington, where they found a Company of our Militia in Arms, upon whom they fired without any provocation and killed 6 Men & wounded 4 others — By an express from Boston we find another Brigade are now upon their March from Boston, supposed to be about 1000 — The Bearer Israel Bissel is charged to alarm the Country quite to Connecticut; and all Persons are desired to furnish him with fresh Horses, as they may be needed — I have spoken with several who have seen the dead & wounded —

J. Palmer one of the Committee of S—y —

forwarded from Worcester April 19 1775
Brookline — Thursday 11 o'Clock
Norwich — 4 o'Clock
New London — 7 o'Clock
Lyme — Friday Morning 1 o'Clock
Saybrook — 4 o'Clock
Killingsworth — 7 o'Clock
E Guilford — 8 o'Clock
Guilford — 10 o'Clock
Branford — 12 o'Clock
New Haven — April 21st
Rec'd & forwarded on certain Intelligence
Fairfield — April 22 8 o'Clock

Copy of the alarm carried by Israel Bissel. *New York Public Library.*

on Friday, the morning of the twenty-first. Johnson's neighbor John McCurdy signed Bissel's alarm as a member of Lyme's Committee of Correspondence, and the minuteman continued his frantic ride down the coast, crossing the Connecticut River and arriving in Saybrook at

4:00 a.m., Killingworth at 7:00 a.m., Guilford at 10:00 a.m., Branford at noon and New Haven later that day. Bissel continued his ride down the Connecticut coast all day Saturday, and by early Sunday morning, April 23, he had reached the Bowery in New York City, just as the men of Lyme's militia began their march to Lexington.

Between Watertown, Massachusetts, and New York City, Bissel had covered over 240 miles in four days. A good day's journey in 1775 was considered to be 30 miles a day over good roads. Bissel's pace was twice that, riding day and night exposed to the elements, traversing bad roads and crossing multiple major rivers. Even more remarkably, he continued on to Philadelphia, where he arrived at 5:00 p.m. on Monday.

The stunning embarrassment of the British at Lexington—that a small detachment sent to teach the treacherous miscreants of Massachusetts a lesson was met with grapeshot, followed by an organized militia of armed men gathered from localities as far-flung as southern New Hampshire and eastern Connecticut who chased them back to Boston along the Charles River, through Waltham and Watertown, in an ignominious retreat where pride was cast aside in efforts to save hide—was only a precursor of what was in store for the British in New England that summer.

Little did the British suspect that the confidence of the colonists was not the braggadocio of rum-swilling ne'er-do-wells but rather the result of hard-won knowledge gained through more than a century of carving out towns and economies from the wilderness without the help of the mother country.

These Americans had negotiated treaties or fought wars against native populations; raised a labor force; established governments, courts, roads and ports; fended off disease and pestilence, wolves and other predators; and dealt with harsh weather that included frigid cold, heavy snow, sweltering summers, floods and droughts. Amid these hardships, they built prosperous towns with bustling commerce and raised militias to defend themselves against invaders foreign and domestic. All of this had been accomplished largely without advice, assistance or resources from England. It is for this reason that New Englanders, accustomed to self-rule and self-reliance, were not only bristling at this new attitude of domination from London but also fully confident in their abilities to push back.

By the time Britain took interest in the affairs of America, it was far too late. In Lyme, it was already too late by 1662, when King Charles II granted Connecticut a charter that legalized the autonomy of its government. Though they would officially remain under the domain of the Crown, Connecticut's governor and legislature were the ultimate authority in the colony. Home rule was preserved for the heirs of the Cromwellian project on Connecticut's coast, and they were determined that this would remain forevermore.

To defend themselves, each town established "trained bands," militias made up of organized volunteers who trained on a regular basis and kept locked stores of arms and ammunition on hand for the common defense. The British caused consternation when they took direct control of militias pressed into service in the French and Indian War. While the colonists were used to commanding their own militias, the unintended consequence of the British action was the creation of a cadre of professionally trained soldiers in the colonies. Revolutionary luminaries such as Virginia's George Washington, Israel Putnam and the Norwich Son of Liberty John Durkee were veterans of the French and Indian War. In Lyme, men such as Elisha Miller and Zebulon Butler also served in both struggles.

When the men of Lyme marched to Lexington in April 1775, they were not going there on a lark. Having driven the British back along the Charles River to Cambridge and then over the river back to the fort in Boston, they did not consider that a victory in and of itself and congratulate themselves on a job well done, satisfied in their accomplishment with stories to tell when they returned to the farm. Rather, they stayed in Massachusetts, and by that

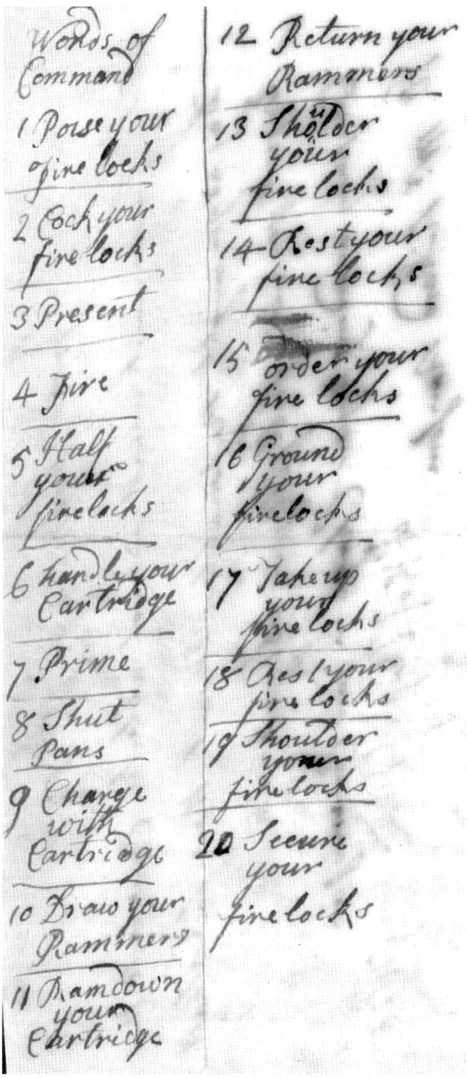
Words of Command
1 Poise your fire locks
2 Cock your fire locks
3 Present
4 Fire
5 Half your firelocks
6 handle your Cartridge
7 Prime
8 Shut Pans
9 Charge with Cartridge
10 Draw your Rammers
11 Ramdown your Cartridge
12 Return your Rammers
13 Sholder your fire locks
14 Rest your fine locks
15 order your fire locks
16 Ground your firelocks
17 Take up your fire locks
18 Rest your fire locks
19 Shoulder your fire locks
20 Secure your fire locks

Militia training commands, Lyme, 1775. *Lyme Historical Society Archives, Florence Griswold Museum.*

summer, a camp would be established in Cambridge that would serve as the headquarters of George Washington, the new commander of the Continental army—an American army that had been forged together from the steely resolves of local militias and placed under his command. It was an authority through popular acclaim, based on the will of the people and confirmed by their representatives in the Continental Congress. The British would never set foot in Cambridge again. And soon, they would be driven from Boston entirely.

Chapter 9

SAMUEL HOLDEN PARSONS

Lyme's Major General

Men of America, citizens of this great country hanging upon the precipice of war, loyalty to England lies behind you, broken by the acts of the mother country—a cruel mother, deaf to the voice of liberty and right; duty to freedom, duty to your country, duty to God is before you; your patriotism is brought to the test; I call upon those ready to volunteer for the defense of the provinces against British tyranny to step into the broad isle.

—Reverend Jonathan Parsons

These were the words that Reverend Jonathan Parsons spoke to his parishioners at the Old South Presbyterian Church in Newburyport on the eve of the Battle of Bunker Hill, urging the young men in his congregation to step into the center aisle of the church and volunteer to take up arms against Britain. Since leaving Lyme and taking up the pastorate at Newburyport in 1745, Parsons had become one of the nation's most famous and powerful clergymen. This avatar of the New Lights, who along with George Whitefield led the charge to reform New England's Congregational Church, had seen the movement evolve from a spiritual to a political movement.

Parsons's brother-in-law, Matthew Griswold IV, had become one of the leading New Light leaders in Connecticut's general assembly, and Griswold was now serving as deputy governor of the Colony of Connecticut under New Light governor Jonathan Trumbull. Griswold and Trumbull, proponents of the political autonomy of Connecticut, were now fully committed Revolutionaries calling for American independence.

The evangelist George Whitefield, who had come to join his friend Parsons at the influential Old South Church, had passed away in 1770 and was buried in the church crypt. Jonathan Parsons himself was nearing the end of his life. Within a year, just after the signing of the Declaration of Independence, he would be laid to rest in the same tomb as Whitefield, under the Old South pulpit. But now, with war at hand, the seventy-year-old Revolutionary cleric was summoning up his storied oratorical powers one last time to call America's young men to battle. His own son, Samuel Holden Parsons, had already answered the call.

The younger Parsons had set out for Boston at the first Lexington alarm in April. Now, as his father was exhorting his parish to rebellion, Samuel was already returning to Boston as the leader of the Sixth Connecticut Regiment. Colonel Samuel Holden Parsons brought with him Lyme's Reverend Stephen Johnson, who enlisted in the regiment with the Lexington alarm and was now serving as its chaplain. Johnson, author of the incendiary anti–Stamp Act pamphlets, was the elder Parsons's successor in the Lyme ministry. Though not as flamboyant as his predecessor, he was even more dedicated to the New Light cause. Though not a young man, the fifty-one-year-old Johnson committed himself body and soul to the cause of independence by marching with Colonel Parsons. Also marching with the Sixth Regiment was Colonel Parsons's own son, Billy, just twelve years of age. On the eve of Bunker Hill, three generations of Parsons men and Lyme's current minister were prepared to challenge the British Empire not just in word but also in deed.

Samuel Holden Parsons was nine years old when his father left Lyme to take up the ministry at Newburyport. By the age of fifteen, he had entered Harvard College, where his classmates included John Hancock, John Adams and Jonathan Trumbull, who became lifelong friends and fellow Revolutionaries. But growing up in Lyme and seeing the Great Awakening firsthand made a lasting impression on the young Parsons, and he soon returned to his family's roots.

After graduating from Harvard at nineteen, Samuel Holden returned to Lyme to study law under his uncle Matthew Griswold IV. One of Connecticut's leading attorneys, Griswold not only taught Samuel law but also gave him access to the center of political power in the colony. Matthew Griswold represented one of the oldest and most powerful families on the coast, and his wife, Ursula Wolcott Griswold, was probably the most politically connected woman in the entire colony. Though often said in terms of bemusement that would seem to indicate exaggeration, it was, in fact, true that Ursula's father, brother, husband, son, nephew and four of her cousins had been governors of Connecticut. Further cementing ties among the colony's elite, Samuel Holden married Mehetable Mather in September 1761.

The Mathers were one of Lyme's founding families and among the earliest English settlers in America. Samuel's wedding to Mehetable, held at her father Richard's mansion on Mather's Neck, was one of the legendary social events of the era. Located where today's Amtrak railroad enters Old Lyme on the east bank of the Connecticut River, the wedding party at Mather's Neck was so large that it took a full barrel of flour to make the wedding cake.

At the age of twenty-four, Samuel Holden Parsons had it all. He was a successful attorney, politically connected and happily married. There was no doubt that he would become one of the colony's luminaries, but in 1761, no one could have guessed just how brightly his star would shine and that his life would be so inextricably intertwined with the birth of a new nation.

Following in his uncle Matthew Griswold's footsteps, Samuel Holden Parsons was elected to the Connecticut General Assembly in 1762, at the age of twenty-five. He would be reelected to twelve consecutive terms and serve in the assembly until 1774.

In keeping with his family's political sympathies, the patriotic Parsons was appointed to the Standing Committee of Correspondence by the general assembly in May 1773. The committee was charged with communicating with other colonies on matters of mutual defense, those matters primarily consisting of resistance to British authority. In November, he was appointed prosecuting attorney for New London County. He joined the Connecticut militia the following year as a major in the Third Regiment, based in Lyme and New London. On April 26, 1775, just after the Lexington alarm, the general assembly called a special session and raised six regiments of Connecticut troops for defense of the state and neighboring colonies against the threat of British invasion. Parsons was made colonel on May 1, 1775, and appointed head of the Sixth Regiment, based in New London. Three days after the Lexington alarm, Parsons set out from New London as part of the old Third Regiment and remained in Massachusetts for thirty days. He returned to New London to take command of the newly formed Sixth Regiment but, only a few short weeks later, on June 7, 1775, was ordered back to Boston by Governor Jonathan Trumbull.

Boston being a five- or six-day march, Parsons would have arrived there a few days before the battle at Bunker Hill on June 17. The battle had been

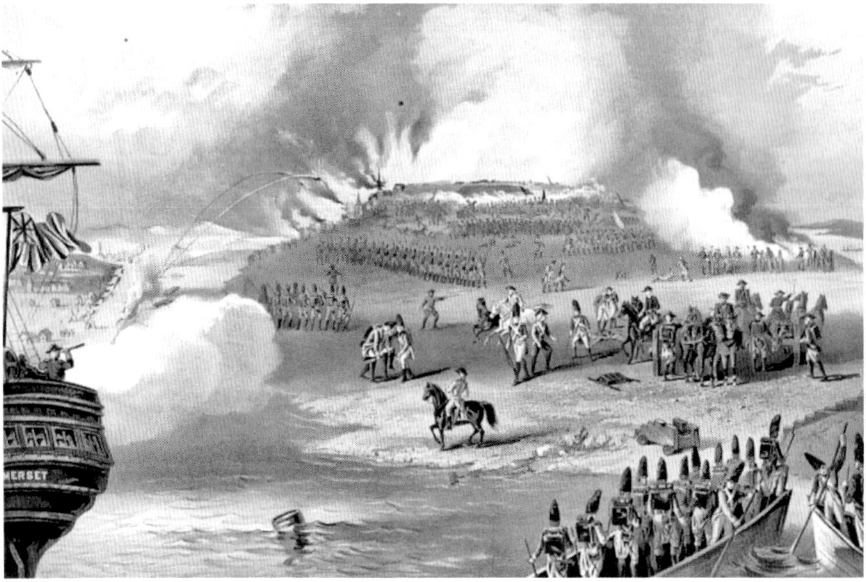

The Battle at Bunker's Hill, Henry A. Thomas. *Library of Congress Prints and Photographs Division.*

brewing for some time. The British were occupying the city of Boston and blockading the harbor. Americans held the hills outside the city: Charlestown to the north and Dorchester to the south. British plans to extend their line and occupy Charlestown had become known, and seeking to head them off, the Americans occupied and began fortifying the hills on June 16. By the seventeenth, they had dug in and were girded for battle. British forces crossed the Mystic River from Boston and landed at Charlestown at noon, expecting that the most formidable, supplied and well-trained army in the world would make short work of this ragtag assembly of rebel militias and once and for all put an end to the insurrection.

The bloodbath that ensued shocked the British and, in contemporary accounts, served to shake the very foundations of their confidence, not only in their invincibility, but also in their own cause. The battle raged for the better part of the day, with heavy casualties on both sides. The British were not prepared for the vehemence of the resistance. The British commander, General Howe, made two attempts to flank the fort at the rail fence that led from the hill to the Mystic River, but he was repelled twice. Parsons's regiment held the line behind that rail fence.

William Coit's company, part of Parsons's regiment, suffered heavy casualties. Parsons's own company survived without serious losses, the only casualty being John Saunders of Lyme, whose wounds were not life-threatening. Parsons wrote a full account of the battle to his uncle, Deputy Governor Matthew Griswold, but that letter has unfortunately been lost to history. A surviving letter to his wife, Mehetable, written two days after the battle, gives a sense of the day:

> *The whole loss on our side not yet ascertained, but I think it will not fall short of 130 killed or wounded. We are raising batteries and should soon be able to do their work if we had powder sufficient, which at present I fear. Many suppose the number of their troops exceed our expectations which must be the case if their number of tents are not for a deception which I suspect it to be. They fought bravely, were twice repulsed by our men and rallied again and forced our intrenchments sword in hand. We have had nothing but a few scattering shot here since Sunday. I am pretty well over the fatigue of Saturday night which I spent on the soft side of a rock on my arms, amidst a cloud of bombs and cannon balls, but thanks to God but two men were killed and about the same number wounded. Billy is well; he is gone to Newbury to-day to buy me some things, as nothing is to be had here. I intend to keep him out of danger if I can.*

When the year 1775 dawned, Samuel Holden Parsons was one of Connecticut's most successful attorneys, earning the princely sum of $2,000 a year. He had a large estate in Lyme, with a loving wife and a large family. The twelve-term assemblyman had been appointed to high office in the colony, and with his father a leading figure in the religious and political community of Massachusetts and his uncle and mentor serving as deputy governor of Connecticut, it stretches the imagination to think that a few short months later this exemplar of power and privilege would himself take up arms and march to Boston to confront the British troops. By the summer, this Harvard lawyer and son of a minister would be sleeping on his gun, on the "soft side of a rock," with bullets and cannonballs flying overhead. In a most unlikely turn, Samuel Holden Parsons would spend the next seven years of his life serving in the war, crisscrossing the Northeast, rising to the rank of major general, becoming one of Washington's most trusted men and engaging in the American Revolution's most iconic battles.

On June 15, just before the Battle of Bunker Hill, George Washington was appointed commander in chief of the Continental troops by the Continental Congress in Philadelphia. By July 2, Washington arrived at

Cambridge to take command of the troops at Boston. Though the British controlled Boston and Charlestown, the Americans held the Charles River west of Boston and the hills of Roxbury to the south. Parsons's regiment was in the camps at Roxbury, preparing for the next battle. Though the two sides were entrenched in their lines through the summer, ready for the call to fire, that call never came. Save for a few small skirmishes, the summer slowly turned to autumn, and the battle was more one of nerves than blood. With winter closing in, wearying of the constant state of readiness with no action, the diarist Samuel Bixby wrote, "[A] flag of truce was sent into Boston by Colonel Parsons and one was returned by the enemy." As the snow began to fall, both sides could now stand at ease and dig in for the harsh Boston winter.

Bunker Hill broke British resolve. While the war against the Americans would continue for eight years and grow more savage, it seemed clear to many in London that the war was lost. That winter, King George III tried and failed to raise twenty thousand additional British and Irish troops to fight in America. He turned to Russia's Catherine the Great for support, but she refused to supply him troops, with a cutting remark that not only made it clear Russia would not defend Britain's empire but also underscored the illegitimacy of George III as the sire of Britain: "Could not his Majesty make use of Hanoverians?"

In the end, George did have to turn to his relations on the Continent, paying German princes to supply him with mercenary troops to fight his colonial war. While Hessians would do Britain's dirty work, the soldiers of the American cause were unique. They were not just farmers and peasants and journeymen—they also counted among their ranks the educated, powerful and wealthy. Their leaders were not sitting back in smug comfort and safety, sending other men's sons to war; they were marching, accompanied by their own sons, and prepared to sacrifice their own flesh, blood and treasure for the cause. It was this factor that remains striking to this day and underscores the power and truth of their conviction. At the time, the British underestimated this dedication on the part of America's elite, and they understandably found it completely inconceivable that America's leading politicians would not only vote for war but also lead the charge into the breach themselves, pay for it out of pocket and bring their young sons with them. This was the intangible element that struck down the power of the British Empire.

That winter was dedicated to planning. When the rivers thawed in the spring of 1776, a fresh attack was planned against the British. On March 4, Washington's troops took Dorchester Heights. Heavy weather prevented British counterattack, and by the next day, American forces were in such a formidable position that the British ceded the southern hills overlooking Boston. By March 16, Washington had taken control of the road along the narrow isthmus between Roxbury and Boston and prepared to close in on the city itself. The events of the next day were the one thing that the Americans had not foreseen or planned for that winter: on March 17, the British gave up and evacuated Boston. The surrender of Boston was complete. No foreign troops, including British troops, have ever set foot on Massachusetts soil again, from March 17, 1776, to the present day. That March 17 was Saint Patrick's Day was lost on no one, as noted by contemporary accounts, and continues to resonate as an undertone of that city's famed celebrations to this day.

While Howe's troops went to Halifax, it was clear that they were not abandoning America altogether but regrouping with other designs in mind. Washington immediately began moving his army to New York, and on April 4, 1776, Samuel Holden Parsons, by now the commander of the Tenth, Seventeenth and Twentieth Foot Regiments, received his orders to move his men from Boston to New York and join Spencer's brigade there. Washington's marching orders to Parsons underscored the esteem Lyme's attorney had earned in Boston: "The General, confiding in your zeal, experience, and good conduct, is satisfied that no vigilance will be wanting on your part."

Washington and Parsons could also truly be called "brothers in arms." Like Samuel Adams, the Marquis de Lafayette, John Hancock, Benjamin Franklin and many of the other luminaries of the Revolution, George Washington and Samuel Holden Parsons were both Freemasons.

The plotting of the Revolution took place in the Masonic lodges of the colonies. The Sons of Liberty were recruited and organized within the ranks of Freemasonry, and meetings were held in taverns associated with the craft, such as the Green Dragon in Boston. The craft was long established and influential in Boston. The first documented Masonic lodge in America was established there in 1733, one year before Benjamin Franklin helped found Philadelphia's lodge. Receiving its charter from the Grand Lodge of England, Boston's St. John's Lodge was the first in a line that included Newport Lodge, established in 1749; New Haven's Hiram Lodge, founded in 1750; New London's, in 1753; and Middletown's, in 1754. A second tradition of Masonry was also founded in Boston with the establishment of St. Andrew's Lodge in 1754. St. Andrews received its charter from the Grand Lodge of Scotland, and subsequent lodges in this line included some in Connecticut, such as Colchester (1781) and Norwich (1785). The two traditions of Masonry arising from the two Grand Lodges of Boston, one English and one Scottish, continue to mark the variations in ritual between

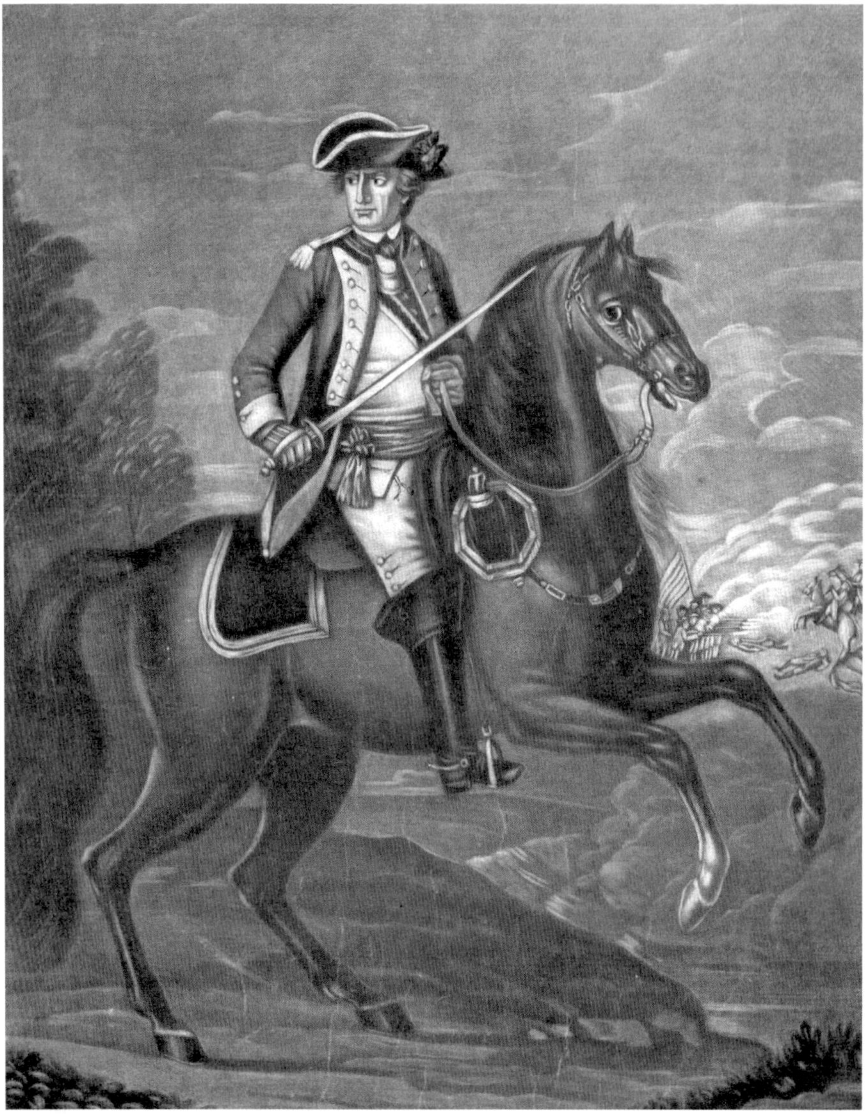

General George Washington. *New York Public Library.*

individual lodges in Connecticut to the present day. The two traditions were officially united under the Grand Lodges of Connecticut and Massachusetts after the Revolution, but those founded before the establishment of those Grand Lodges were permitted to keep their unique rituals.

What the Masonic lodge offered its members was mutual aid—assistance in times of distress and help for the widows and orphans of brothers who met untimely fates. It offered social connections and opportunities, safe havens in unfamiliar towns, a network of brothers throughout Europe and the Americas who were bound to each other by oath and could be recognized by subtle signals and passwords. Utilizing a universal symbolism communicated through images and gestures, Masons could operate and receive protection in unfamiliar lands and prove their credentials even when they were unfamiliar with the language. For American merchants and entrepreneurs, the Masonic lodge was an important institution that helped members operate across borders, do business in unfamiliar places and forge bonds with like-minded individuals in other countries. When Lafayette first

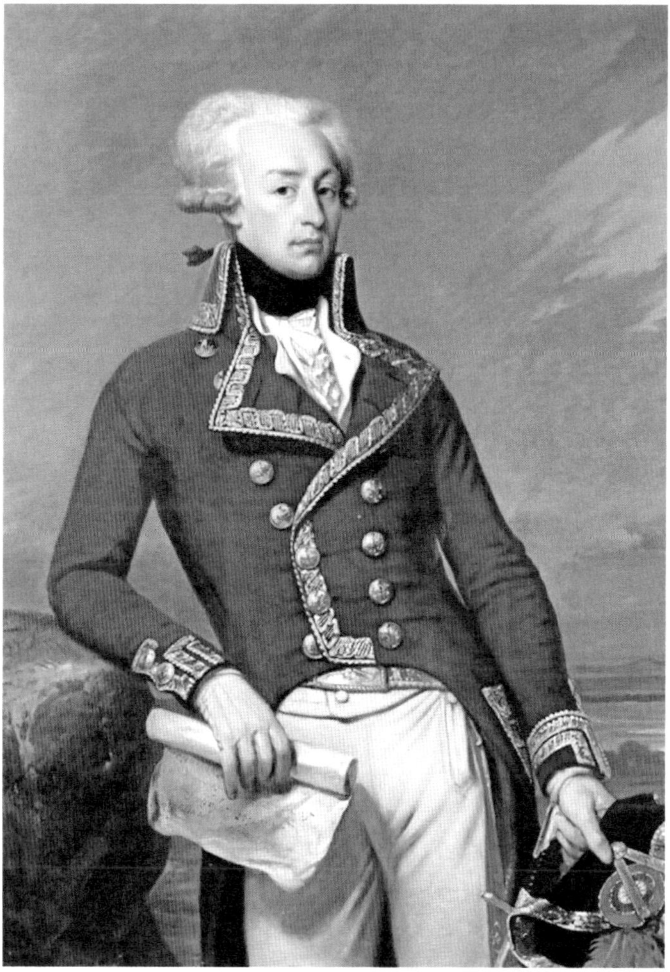

Gilbert du Motier, Marquis de Lafayette. *Portrait by Joseph Désiré Court.*

arrived in Philadelphia to offer Congress his services in the cause of the American Revolution, he was rebuffed as a mercenary adventurer. But when he then sent a signal to the brothers within that he was a fellow Freemason, Lafayette was immediately given audience, and learning of his zeal for the cause and willingness to fund his own expedition, Congress made the noble-born Frenchman the youngest general in the Continental army.

The Battle of Bunker Hill, and the long siege of Boston that followed, disrupted the regular working of Boston's Grand Lodge, and meetings were eventually suspended. Masonic lodges were charter-bound to meet on certain days and at regular intervals, and brothers were expected to attend most, if not all, of the stated and summoned communications. With most able-bodied men now in the camps of the Continental army, a new lodge was founded with a special dispensation stating that it did not have to meet in a specific time and place. The American Union Lodge was chartered in Boston in April 1776 as a traveling lodge of the Continental army.

Among its first members was Samuel Holden Parsons, who is listed as a Fellowcraft in the lodge's first rolls. Other members of the Connecticut line included Israel Putnam, the Sixth Regiment's William Coit and Lyme's Elisha Ely. By 1779, Parsons is listed as Worshipful Master of the Lodge, which was then meeting at Nelson Point, New York, where Parsons's regiment was stationed.

The founding of the lodge coincided with the movement of the army out of Boston in the spring of 1776. Washington made his way from his headquarters at Cambridge to New York City via Norwich, New London and Lyme. His journey is remembered for its solemnity. The striking image of the general riding his white steed, coming down the Mohegan Road from Norwich to New London, silently nodding at the gathered multitudes regarding him in awe, is mentioned in numerous contemporary accounts. In New London, on April 9, he stayed with Nathaniel Shaw, master of numerous ships that would be pressed into service as privateers in the war against the British navy. Leaving New London and making his way to Lyme, Washington avoided the Post Road, due to its crossing at the Rope Ferry—his horse was famously averse to crossing water—and passed instead at the headwaters of the Niantic River, stopping at the Caulkins Tavern on the way. Washington spent April 10 in Lyme, staying overnight at the home of John McCurdy, a man who had proven himself a true Son of Liberty. No doubt Washington was just as impressed by McCurdy's abilities as a merchant. In addition to his store and docks at Lyme, McCurdy had purchased a wharf, warehouse and mansion in New London also, approximately at the place

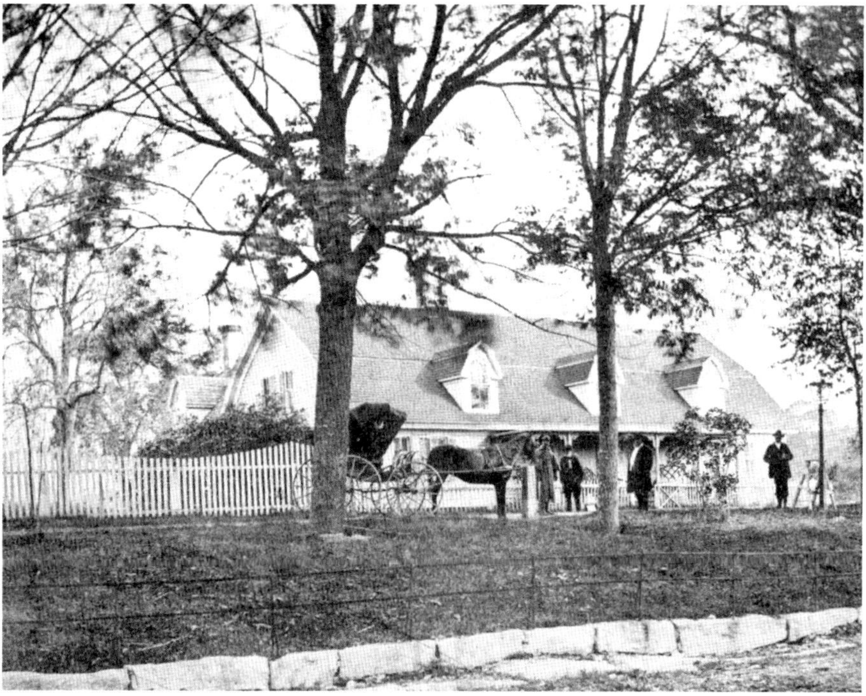

Caulkins Tavern, circa 1890, Flanders Four Corners, East Lyme. Washington and Lafayette both stopped here for refreshment. *Courtesy of the East Lyme Historical Society.*

where Golden Street meets Bank Street. He owned many merchant vessels that could prove critical in the coming war.

By the end of April, over ten thousand Continental troops, most of them from New England, were occupying New York City. Samuel Holden Parsons was serving under General Spencer and camped at what is now the Lower East Side of Manhattan, near Madison and Rutgers Streets. Over the next two months, 130 ships of the English fleet arrived and anchored off Sandy Hook. General Howe, who had evacuated Boston and brought his army to Halifax, was now on Staten Island. By the end of July, the British fleet was 400 ships strong, and in August, Howe was joined by Generals Clinton and Cornwallis, plus the Hessian troops. By the end of August, Britain's forces numbered thirty-one thousand men, including eight thousand Hessian mercenaries. A showdown between the British and the Americans in New York was now inevitable. Against Britain's thirty-one thousand troops, Washington had mustered twenty-eight thousand at his command, but of those, only about nineteen thousand were prepared for duty. Undertrained and underequipped to begin with, the American ranks were also decimated by disease tearing through the camps. On August 4, Parsons wrote, "My doctor and mate are sick. I have nearly two hundred men sick in camp; my neighbors are in very little better state."

Parsons, though, enjoyed the full faith and confidence of his fellow Patriots. On August 4, 1776, John Adams wrote, "A general officer ought to be a gentleman of letters and general knowledge, a man of address and knowledge of the world. He should carry with him authority and command. There are among the New England officers gentlemen who are equal to all this: Parsons, Hitchcock, Varnum, and others." Parsons's old Harvard friend John Hancock wrote a letter to him a week later, on August 10, informing him that he was being promoted to the rank of brigadier general in the "Army of the American States." By the end of August, that army, led by Brigadier General Samuel Holden Parsons, would find itself in the midst of a brutal battle for the control of New York and Long Island.

On August 22, General Howe landed fifteen thousand British troops in Brooklyn, on the southwestern corner of Long Island, and occupied the flatlands south of the ridge of hills that are today's Prospect Park and Greenwood Cemetery.

These hills are a geological feature known as a "terminal moraine," the line where the glaciers made their southernmost advance during the Ice Age. South of this is a sandy outwash plain that forms today's Brooklyn neighborhoods of Flatbush, Kensington, Bensonhurst, Gravesend and Flatlands. While the British occupied the sandy lowlands, the Americans held the hills and blocked the four passes through them: the Narrows Road into Gowanus on the west; the Bedford and the Flatbush Roads in the center; and the Jamaica Road leading up from the shores of Queens on the east. In answer to Howe's landing, Washington ordered regiments from Parsons's brigade to Long Island on August 22. That same day, Washington named Connecticut's Israel Putnam commander of the Long Island forces, and Parsons was given command of Huntington's, Wyllys's, Tyler's, Stillman's, Chester's, Gay's and Ward's regiments.

The first shots were fired on August 27, and Parsons led his regiments to the edge of the hills, repelling British advances on the heights. Parsons's men stormed what is now known as "Battle Hill" in Greenwood Cemetery, near the spot where the statue of Minerva now stands, saluting the Statue of Liberty in New York Harbor.

The fighting was heavy and fierce, in many cases hand-to-hand, but the three hundred men in Parsons's brigade held the commanding heights against two thousand British troops. Parsons had full confidence that he and his men would prevail until he heard shots being fired behind him and saw the hills being stormed from the north. Unknown to Parsons, the American commander Lord Sterling had fallen back on the Narrows Road, and the British were now pouring into Gowanus behind Parsons's lines. It had been agreed that Parsons would be informed of any retreat or change of tactics, but word never reached him. Parsons and his men were now being quickly surrounded. The British were also advancing up Jamaica Road, facing little or no resistance. Stranded and doomed, Parsons gathered what was left of his men and scrambled into the heavy woods to try to reach the American lines. There were scores of dead on both sides. Parsons made it back to the American lines alive with seven of his men.

He wrote a bitter account of the battle to his friend John Adams, pinning the blame for the battle's loss on New York and Pennsylvania troops who lacked the courage to face the British. On October 8, he wrote:

> *On the day of the surprise I was on duty, and at the first dawn of the day the guards from the West road near the Narrows, came to my quarters and informed me the enemy were advancing in great numbers on that road. I soon found it true and that the whole guard had fled without firing a gun; these (by way of retaliation I must tell you) were all New Yorkers and Pennsylvanians. I found by fair daylight the enemy were through the wood and descending the hill on the North side, on which with 20 of my fugitive guard being all I could collect, I took a post on the height in their front at about a half mile's distance, which halted their column.*

He went on:

> *I am still of the opinion, if our guards on the West road and Col. Miles on East end of the hills had done their duty, the enemy would not have passed those important heights, without such very great loss as would have obliged them to abandon any further enterprise on the Island.*

Two days later, on August 29, a council of war was held at Philip Livingstone's home, near the corner of Hicks and Joralemon Streets in Brooklyn. Washington presided over the council, which included Major Generals Putnam and Spencer and Brigadier Generals Wadsworth, McDougall, Mifflin, Scott, Fellows and Parsons. It was agreed that the Americans could not hold Long Island, and Parsons was appointed to coordinate a retreat that night. In what is still considered today one of the most masterful military maneuvers in history, Parsons commanded

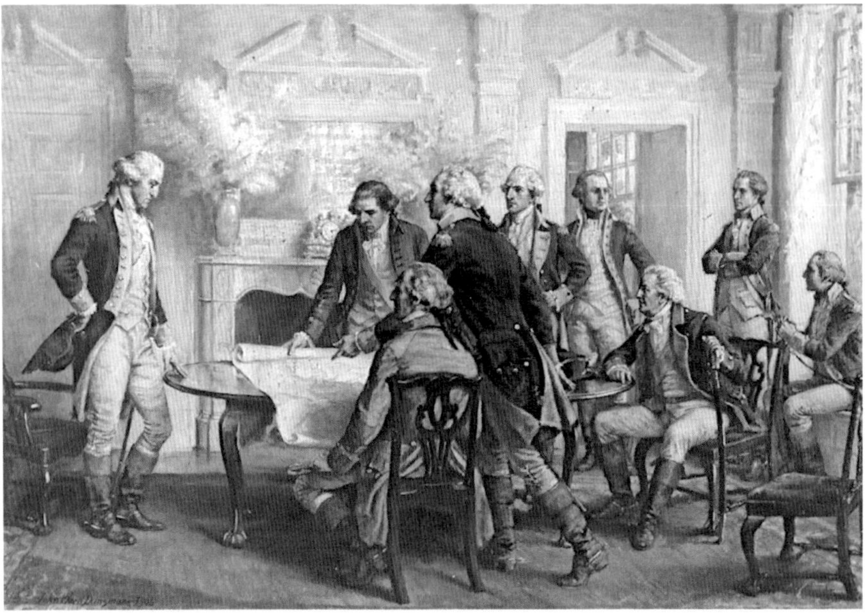

John Ward Dunsmore, *Conference of Washington and His Generals after the Battle of Long Island. Left to right*: Washington, Parsons, Spencer, Mifflin, Scott, McDougall, Putnam, Wadsworth and Fellows. *From* The Refugees of 1776 from Long Island to Connecticut *by Frederic G. Mather.*

the retreat of the entire American force without detection by the British. Beginning in the rain, just after dark on the night of the twenty-ninth, the evacuation of Long Island continued through the heavy fog until dawn, as rowboat after rowboat carried a total of at least nine thousand men across the East River from Brooklyn Ferry to Manhattan.

Parsons and his men took positions on Manhattan's eastern shore, guarding the coast from Corlear's Hook to today's Fifteenth Street. From there he could observe the British fleet in the East River. But rather than idly waiting for a British attack, Parsons would instead play a key role in the execution of a historic plan involving a new military invention. Parsons's friend from Saybrook, David Bushnell, had invented the submarine. The Yale inventor was certain his submarine could be positioned undetected under the British fleet, where its pilot would attach explosives to a ship's hull and blow the vessel out of the water. When Bushnell's trained and trusted pilot, his brother Ezra, fell ill in camp and was unable to pilot the machine, he needed to find a capable, courageous fellow to operate the vessel, and quickly. For this, he turned to Samuel Parsons. Parsons knew just the man for the job. He chose one under his command, whom he had known much of his life: his own brother-in-law, Ezra Lee.

Chapter 10

EZRA LEE AND THE AMERICAN *TURTLE*

Of all the wild schemes, harebrained experiments and crazy notions that possessed America in the eighteenth century, perhaps none was as far-fetched, bold and very nearly successful as the attempt to blow up the British fleet at New York with a new invention: the submarine.

In an era when aged philosophers flew kites in thunderstorms and lawyers and ministers took up arms to fight the world's most powerful army, David Bushnell's invention, the *Turtle*, the world's first submarine, stands out as an audacious project that was overshadowed only by the bravery of Lyme's Ezra Lee, who consented to pilot the submersible vessel under New York's East River, targeting the English fleet docked there in the midst of a rout that sent the American army scrambling in retreat. Lee's aim was to position the *Turtle* undetected under one of His Majesty's ships and attach explosives to the hull in an attempt to blow the English warship out of the water, so demoralizing and panicking the British navy that they would be forced to abandon the port of New York entirely. These specialized explosives, capable of detonating under water, had also been invented by Bushnell. The fact that this scheme very nearly succeeded mere days after the defeat of American troops in the Battle of Long Island is one of the most daring episodes in the War of Independence.

Born in 1740 in Saybrook, just across the river from Lyme, David Bushnell was completing his final year at Yale and preparing for graduation when the first shots were fired at Lexington in 1775. At Yale, Bushnell gravitated toward science, or "natural philosophy" as it was called, and specialized in

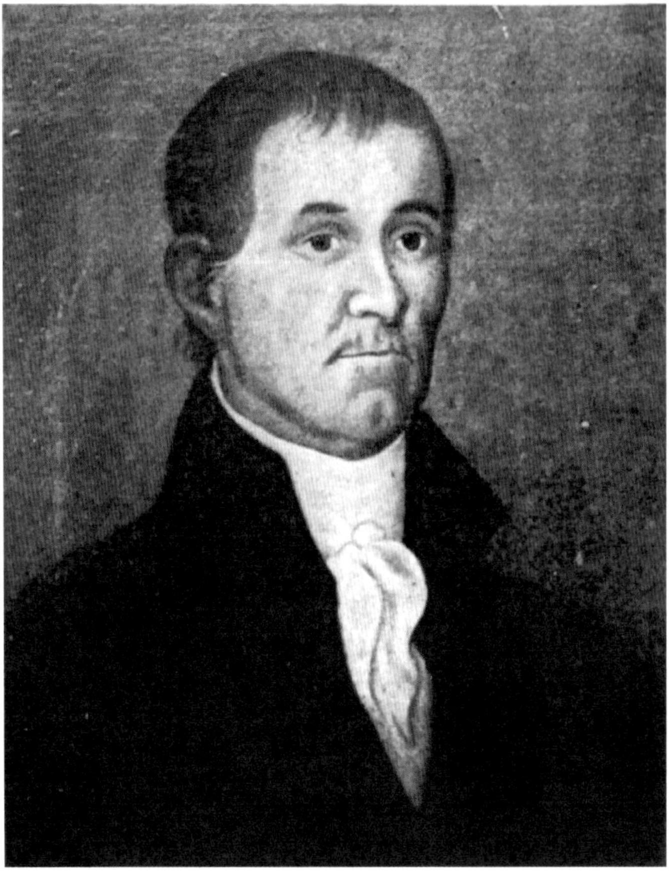

Ezra Lee was the pilot of Bushnell's *Turtle*, the first submarine used in combat. *From* The Story of the Submarine *by Farnham Bishop.*

experimenting with underwater explosives. His attempts to explode these "torpedoes" or "sea mines" sent both metaphorical and literal shockwaves through Yale's campus and into the streets of New Haven beyond. It was feared that the eccentric inventor was bound to kill someone or die trying.

But when war broke out in nearby Lexington, the patriotic heart of the Saybrook native focused his scientific mind to apply these theoretical, albeit dramatic, experiments in underwater explosives to an invention that could be used to advance the American cause. What if one could attach an explosive undetected to the hull of a ship and, in so doing, use the element of surprise to change the very nature of maritime warfare? With the Patriot-controlled Connecticut River as his home base for experimentation, Bushnell set to work and perfected not only the detonation of gunpowder under water but

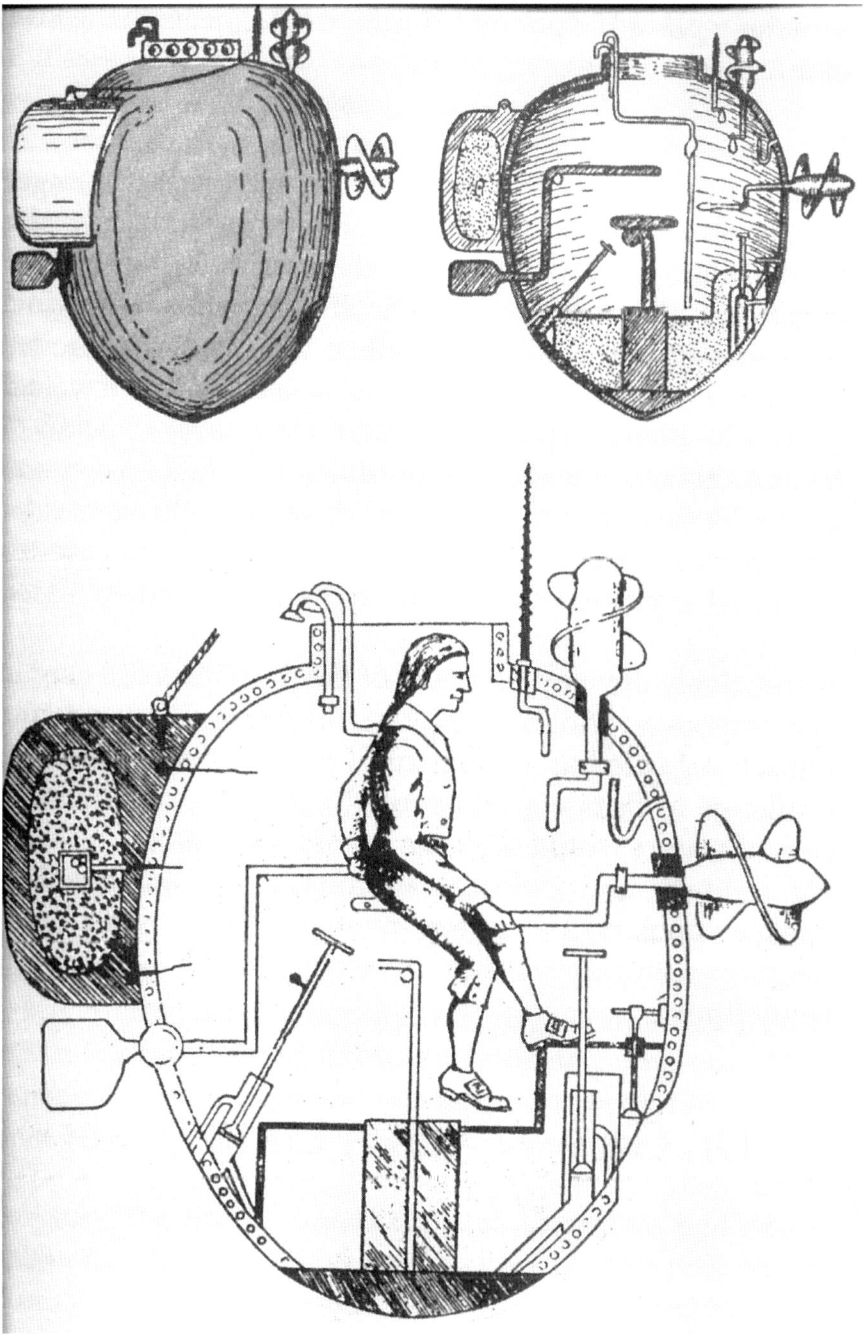

Nineteenth-century depiction of Bushnell's *Turtle*. *Library of Congress, Prints and Photographs Division.*

also the means to deliver that charge undetected below a target. With this vision, in 1776, David Bushnell revolutionized the technology of warfare.

The *Turtle* was so named because it was thought to resemble two turtle shells fused together. Bushnell's invention was an oblong sphere constructed of oak, sealed with pitch and bound by iron hoops, much like a glorified keg.

Inside, the operator sat in confined quarters and operated the vessel with a series of controls, propelling it with foot pedals and hand cranks, and raising and lowering it with a series of valves and pumps. Completing the outlandish, yet brilliant, invention was a detachable mine and drilling screw with which the hull of an enemy ship could be compromised and the detachable mine attached thereupon to do its patriotic duty.

The *Turtle* married two innovations: underwater explosions and subsurface navigation. Through early 1776, Bushnell conducted trials off Lyme's Poverty Island, a stone's throw from Deputy Governor Griswold's home and where it was said that Benjamin Franklin himself came to witness the sea trials of this new weapon. Perfecting the invention was a luxury no one could afford, as fear of spies and detection by the British haunted their every step. Just days after the Americans were defeated in Brooklyn and evacuated Long Island, the call came. The experiments were over. The *Turtle* would be pressed into war service.

The original plan was for the *Turtle* to be deployed earlier that summer, but its pilot, David Bushnell's brother Ezra, fell ill and was unable to continue. Samuel Holden Parsons was asked to supply a new volunteer for the mission, and he chose a man from his regiment, his own brother-in-law Ezra Lee. Lee only had two weeks of training, during which time he had to learn how to submerge and raise the submarine, propel it forward, tread water, handle the explosives and operate the screw that would attach the ordnance to the British warship.

The submarine was shipped down the Long Island Sound and then carried overland from New Rochelle to the Hudson River. On September 5, 1776, Samuel Holden Parsons wrote to George Washington, "As all things are now ready to make the experiment, I wish it may not be delayed. Though the event is uncertain, the experiment under our present circumstances is certainly worth trying."

On the night of September 6, Ezra Lee and the *Turtle* were towed by whaleboat as close to General Howe's flagship, HMS *Eagle*, as possible without attracting attention and then cast off. Lee rowed for over two hours, fighting the tide, before he could pull up close to the *Eagle*. In his account, Lee recalled, "[W]hen I rowed under the stern of the ship, I could see men on deck and hear them talk—then I shut all doors, sunk down, and came up under the bottom of the ship, up with the screw against the bottom, but found that it would not enter." Lee repeatedly tried to attach the screw to the hull of the ship, but there was no way to keep the submarine steady while the screw penetrated the ship's bottom. Simultaneously, Lee had to fight the particular push and pull of tides in New York Harbor, almost a complete counterpoint to those at the Connecticut's mouth, and he had no time to parse that equation as he attempted to blow up the world's most formidable navy before dawn. With the eastern skies lightening and daybreak quickly approaching, Lee had to abandon the effort. As he sailed away from the *Eagle*, he was detected by British sailors, who set out to investigate the bizarre craft. Seeing this, Lee said he "let loose the magazine in hopes, that if they should take me, they should likewise pick up the magazine then we should all be blown up together." Luckily for Lee, the ordnance exploded, frightening off the British chase boat and permitting him to escape.

The legacy of the American Revolution is that even in defeat, the heroic seeds of victory can be sown. But with their defeat at Long Island, the American position in New York was tenuous. The British saw New York City as an important pulse point on the American continent and were determined to capture it. While Parsons, Putnam and others held the eastern shores of Manhattan against the British on Long Island for two weeks, on September 15, the British crossed the East River and attacked Manhattan at Kips Bay. The Americans attempted resistance, but in their disorganized state, the Patriots barely managed to escape slaughter at British hands and hastily retreated north. In the mêlée at Kips Bay, Lyme's Colonel Samuel Selden was taken prisoner. A wealthy landowner, lawyer, member of the Connecticut Assembly and veteran of the Siege of Boston, the fifty-two-year-old Samuel Selden had requested and was given command of a regiment on June 20, 1776. By the end of the summer, he was ordered to New York to reinforce American troops there. On July 6, Colonel Selden wrote to Captain Joshua Huntington, imploring him to rally troops for the defense of New York: "Rouse the People to see their Danger. Stir them up by all that is dear in this life. Our Wives, our Children, our property, our Liberty is at Stake."

Selden was not involved in the battle on Long Island. His troops remained in Manhattan, camped at Stuyvesant's Bouwerie Farm in what is today New York City's East Village, charged with the defense of the island's eastern shore. On September 15, less than two weeks after the *Turtle*'s failed attempt to blow the British navy to smithereens, General Howe attacked Manhattan. The fatigued

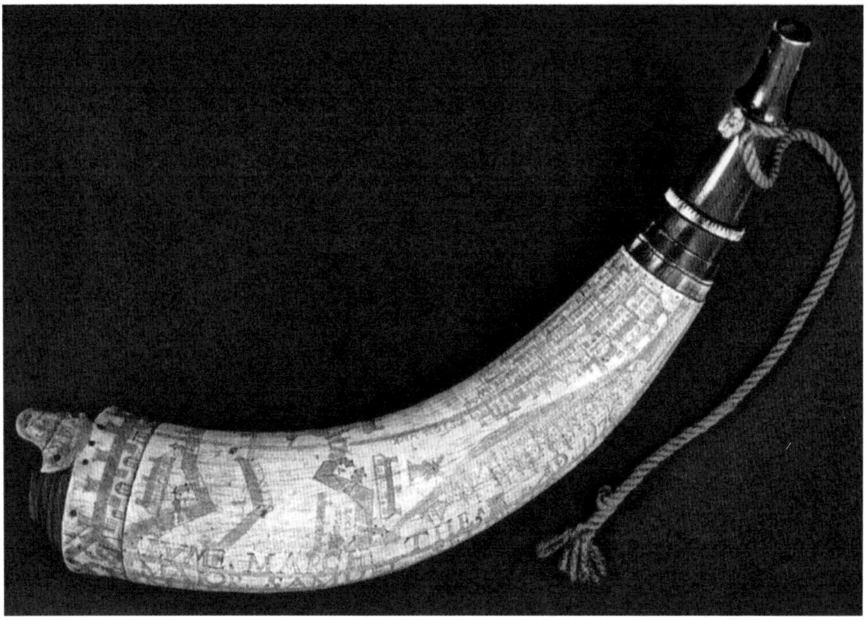

Samuel Selden's powder horn, with "Lyme" etched into the design. *Courtesy of the Massachusetts Historical Society.*

American troops, barely recovered from their retreat from Long Island, put up a defense that was admirable and dispiriting by equal measure.

Replete with crossed signals from command, and with Generals Parsons, Putnam and Washington all present at the head, attempting to rally the troops, the Americans fled in disarray from Howe's attack. Samuel Selden was caught in the confusion. Moving north along the Post Road toward Kips Bay, he and his men encountered Hessian troops at what is today Third Avenue and Twenty-Third Street. Selden and his men put up a worthy defense, killing four Hessian soldiers, but Selden himself was captured and taken prisoner. He was imprisoned at Livingstone's Sugar House, which had served as a debtors' prison. Conditions in the prison, now under British control, were beyond deplorable. Selden was taken ill with fever and moved to the Old Provost prison, where conditions were only marginally better. He died on October 11, 1776, and was esteemed enough by British command that he was afforded the rare distinction of being allowed to be buried with full military honors in the Brick Churchyard. Selden's son Elijah was also serving in New York, under General Parsons at the Battle of Long Island. Luckily, Elijah managed to stay close to Parsons, and both narrowly escaped the pursuing British troops.

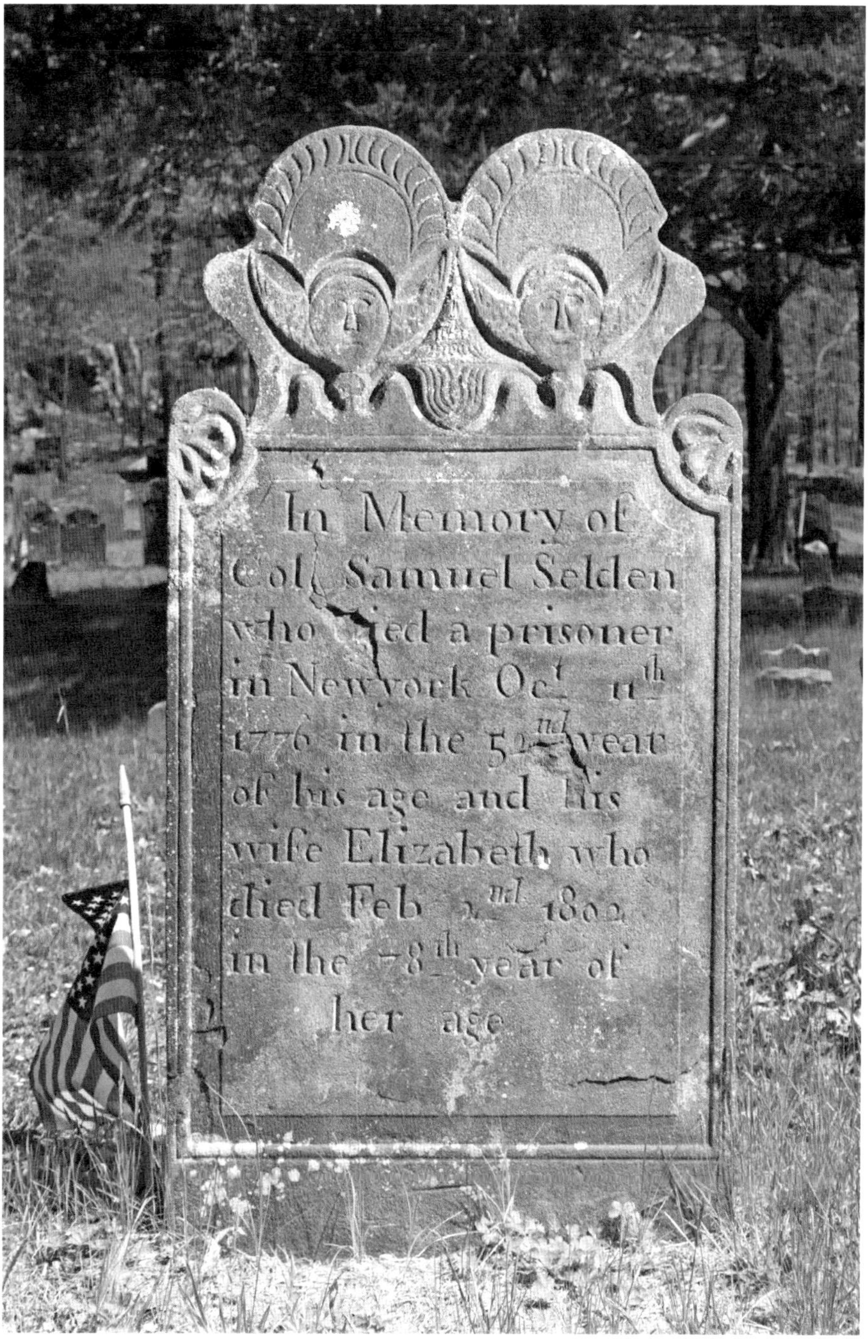

Colonel Samuel Selden's grave marker. *Courtesy of the Lyme Local History Archives/Lyme Public Hall Association, Inc.*

Ezra Lee escaped capture after his first attempt to sink the *Eagle* and attempted his stunt again on October 5, in the Hudson River, but unfortunately met with similar results. A subsequent pilot, Phineas Pratt, also failed in his attempt. By this time, the British were on constant lookout for the *Turtle*. Though it had not yet successfully completed a mission, Bushnell's invention rattled the nerves of the British navy. When, on that first night, the mine that was cut loose exploded in the East River, it finally dawned on the British that these Americans were both brilliant and crazy. It was yet another sign that they could no longer be underestimated.

Chapter 11

The War Comes Home

Dear Thomas—I have sent two soldiers to live at your house. One understands French and the other painting. You may learn something from them. I wish you to remember your books. Be virtuous and manly in your behavior, a comfort to your mother and family. Leave off all childish follies and learn to behave with decency and manly fortitude. Lay aside that bashful conduct. A modest behavior with resolution and courage will endear you to all your acquaintances. Falsehood and lies you must always abhor and detest.

Billy will be home next week. When I shall come home I can't tell, but remember, if I fall in this war, I expect you and all my sons to arm in defense of your glorious liberty and lay down your lives in defense of your country and to avenge my death, if necessary.

—Samuel Holden Parsons in a letter to his nine-year-old-son, Thomas, December 27, 1776

From the moment he received word of the British attack on Lexington in April 1775, Samuel Holden Parsons had been steadily on the battlefield. After fighting at Bunker Hill and the Battle of Long Island, General Parsons was in the thick of the action through the American retreat from New York, fighting at Kips Bay, Harlem Heights and White Plains. Parsons had urged retreat from New York City at the council of war on September 15. His advice was wise, as the Americans were surrounded by the British fleet and in danger of being trapped in New York if they did not retreat. Washington would eventually move his troops up the Hudson River and cross into

New Jersey. Parsons was charged with defending the critical Hudson River crossing at Peekskill and spent a good part of the next year traveling all over New York and Connecticut between the Hudson and Connecticut Rivers following Washington's orders, alternately defending the coast and the highland crossings, which were critical to maintaining supply lines and communications between New England and the rest of the new nation.

As the theater of war moved into the mid-Atlantic, it was essential that the highland crossings be defended if Connecticut's Governor Jonathan Trumbull was to continue supplying food and arms to American forces from New Jersey to Pennsylvania. Trumbull's ability to raise troops and resources, answering Washington's call time and again when others had failed, earned Trumbull the esteem of all Americans and Connecticut the nickname "Provision State." The close relationship between Parsons and his fellow Freemason Trumbull was an essential key to Connecticut's role in support of the Revolution. The steadfast, sober character of General Parsons is revealed in his Christmas 1776 letter to his son Thomas, and his unshaken resolve is evident in all of his letters, in which the possibility of his own death is acknowledged, but the possibility of defeat is never contemplated. Parsons wrote, "That we are embarked in the cause of justice and truth—the cause of God and mankind—is beyond a doubt. That we shall finally succeed, I think equally certain."

The certainty of victory of which Parsons was convinced was not shared by many Americans at the close of 1776. Washington's army was in tactical retreat, the British forces were growing larger and bolder and desertions from the American ranks were becoming epidemic. As the harsh winter closed in, Parsons had lost over half of his three-thousand-man force—underfed, undersupplied and often unclothed and unpaid—to illness or desertion. Time and again, Parsons had to return to Connecticut to raise more troops. Miraculously, the resolute general was always able to find patriotic men to enlist in the cause. On Christmas morning 1776, Washington won his first battle, crossing the Delaware for a surprise attack on the unsuspecting Hessians at Trenton.

The early months of 1777 found Samuel Holden Parsons at home in Lyme for the first time in a year and a half, but he wasted no time in leisure. He spent that winter raising troops throughout Connecticut and, under Washington's orders, overseeing the inoculation of the American army against smallpox.

Parsons, along with Governor Trumbull and General Israel Putnam, was eager to attack Tory strongholds on Long Island, just across the sound from

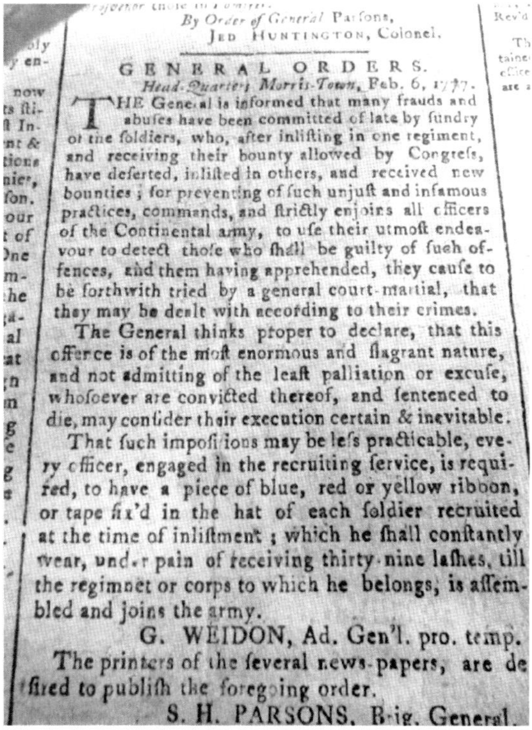

By Order of General Parſons,
JED HUNTINGTON, Colonel.

GENERAL ORDERS.
Head-Quarters Morris-Town, Feb. 6, 1777.

THE General is informed that many frauds and abuſes have been committed of late by ſundry of the ſoldiers, who, after inliſting in one regiment, and receiving their bounty allowed by Congreſs, have deſerted, inliſted in others, and received new bounties; for preventing of ſuch unjuſt and infamous practices, commands, and ſtrictly enjoins all officers of the Continental army, to uſe their utmoſt endeavour to detect thoſe who ſhall be guilty of ſuch offences, and them having apprehended, they cauſe to be forthwith tried by a general court-martial, that they may be dealt with according to their crimes.

The General thinks proper to declare, that this offence is of the moſt enormous and flagrant nature, and not admitting of the leaſt palliation or excuſe, whoſoever are convicted thereof, and ſentenced to die, may conſider their execution certain & inevitable.

That ſuch impoſitions may be leſs practicable, every officer, engaged in the recruiting ſervice, is required, to have a piece of blue, red or yellow ribbon, or tape fix'd in the hat of each ſoldier recruited at the time of inliſtment; which he ſhall conſtantly wear, under pain of receiving thirty-nine laſhes, till the regimnet or corps to which he belongs, is aſſembled and joins the army.

G. WEIDON, Ad. Gen'l. pro. temp.

The printers of the ſeveral news-papers, are deſired to publiſh the foregoing order.

S. H. PARSONS, Brig. General.

Right: Brigadier General Parsons's orders regarding fraud and desertion, *Connecticut Gazette*, 1777. *New London County Historical Society*.

Below: *Connecticut Gazette* advertisement, "Deserted from Col. Selden's Regiment," 1776. *New London County Historical Society*.

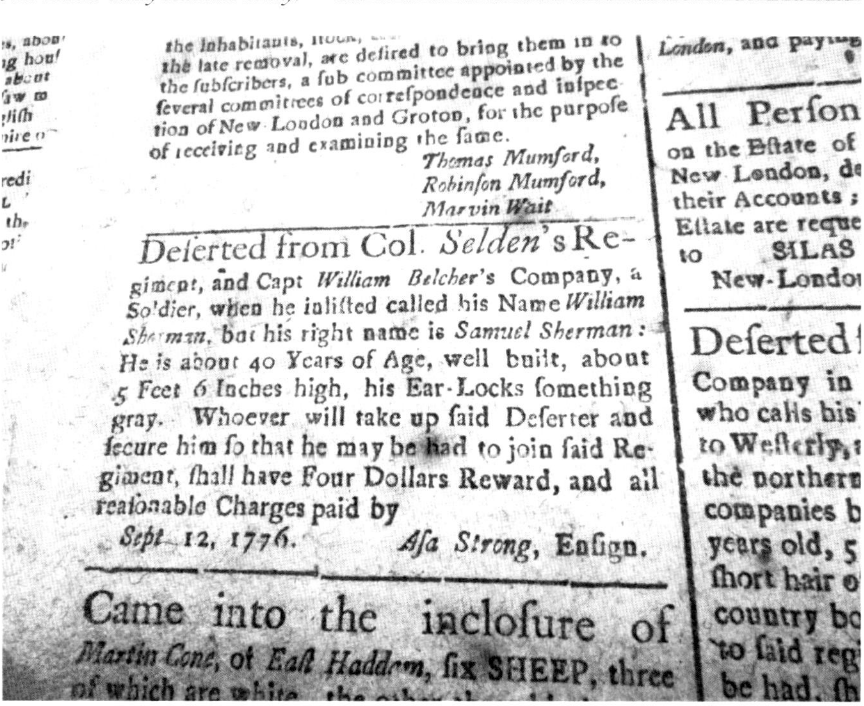

the late removal, are deſired to bring them in to the ſubſcribers, a ſub committee appointed by the ſeveral committees of correſpondence and inſpection of New-London and Groton, for the purpoſe of receiving and examining the ſame.

Thomas Mumford,
Robinſon Mumford,
Marvin Wait.

Deſerted from Col. *Selden's* Regiment, and Capt *William Belcher's* Company, a Soldier, when he inliſted called his Name *William Sherman*, but his right name is *Samuel Sherman*: He is about 40 Years of Age, well built, about 5 Feet 6 Inches high, his Ear-Locks ſomething gray. Whoever will take up ſaid Deſerter and ſecure him ſo that he may be had to join ſaid Regiment, ſhall have Four Dollars Reward, and all reaſonable Charges paid by

Sept. 12, 1776. *Aſa Strong*, Enſign.

Came into the incloſure of *Martin Cone*, of *Eaſt Haddam*, ſix SHEEP, three of which are white ...

All Perſon
on the Eſtate of
New-London, d
their Accounts;
Eſtate are reque
to SILAS
New-Londo

Deſerted
Company in
who calls his
to Weſterly,
the northern
companies b
years old, 5
ſhort hair o
country bo
to ſaid reg
be had, ſh

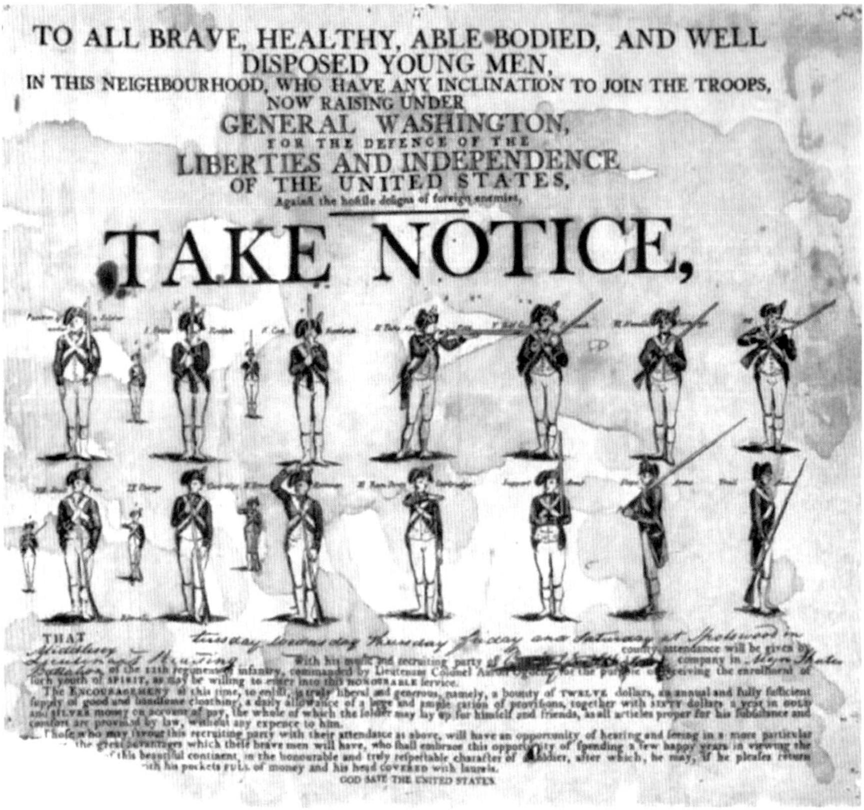

This recruitment poster, circa 1798, is similar to notices that would have been posted during the Revolution to encourage men to enlist. *Connecticut Historical Society.*

Connecticut's coast. Having been born and raised in the coastal town of Lyme, Parsons knew these waters well. On February 16, 1777, he ordered the first attack on Long Island, sending a contingent of twenty whaleboats under the direction of Lyme's Captain Daniel Wait to raid British forage on eastern Long Island that was bound for the army in New York City. Washington was pleased with the success of the raid but reprimanded Wait and his men for looting private property. Parsons then proposed raids on Huntington and Oyster Bay that he would conduct himself, which Washington approved in principle, but with smallpox tearing through the ranks of the American army, the commander in chief ordered Parsons to prioritize the inoculation of the newly raised Connecticut troops, for fear they would infect others.

The boldest and most successful raid on Long Island from Connecticut occurred on May 23, when Parsons ordered an attack on Sag Harbor. Some

170 men in thirteen whaleboats, accompanied by two armed sloops and one unarmed vessel, left Guilford, Connecticut, and landed at Southold, New York, under cover of darkness. Portaging across the north fork of the island, they entered Peconic Bay and rowed to Sag Harbor, surprising the British troops there at 2:00 a.m., attacking the guards, destroying supplies and burning the fleet anchored there. Despite a sustained gun battle, the Americans managed to destroy twelve brigs and sloops; a twelve-gun vessel; 120 tons of pressed oats, hay and other forage; and ten hogsheads of rum. They returned to Connecticut with 90 prisoners. The entire expedition, which covered ninety miles, took a total of twenty-five hours and was accomplished without a single American soldier being lost or wounded.

The success of these raids convinced Governor Trumbull that there should be further attacks on Long Island's Tories, and he advised that some of the new troops raised in Connecticut should remain there to defend the coast and press the war against the English across the sound. Washington disagreed, however, and Parsons sided with Washington, saying that a full-scale attack on the Connecticut coast by the British was unlikely, and the full force of American might would be better deployed in defense of the Hudson River.

Events of the summer of 1777 would prove Washington and Parsons correct. In May, Parsons was ordered to Peekskill, and by June he had joined Washington's forces in New Jersey. Writing to his wife from Bound Brook on June 22, Parsons said, "This state is once more delivered from those pests of society; who will next be infested by them is uncertain, but we are in high spirits, and ready to march to any part of the country."

By July, Parsons was back in Peekskill, holding the crossing with two thousand men and facing the prospect of a terrifying assault. The threat would be realized that autumn, when British general Burgoyne captured Ticonderoga and was pushing down the Hudson toward Albany with eight thousand men. Sir Henry Clinton was coming up the Hudson from New York City with six thousand men, and Lieutenant Colonel St. Leger was arriving with an additional force of one thousand men, mainly Loyalist Canadians and Native Americans from the Mohawk Valley. The main theater of war at this time was outside Philadelphia, where General Howe's troops were engaging Washington's at Germantown and Brandywine. It was at Brandywine that the Marquis de Lafayette first distinguished himself in brave defense of the American cause. But this new threat against the mid-Hudson crossing promised to divide the American forces in two and cut New England off from the rest of the country. Americans could not win this war if access across the Hudson was cut off.

Israel Putnam was commander of the army at Peekskill, and his job grew infinitely more difficult on September 23 when Washington ordered the withdrawal of Continental forces under Putnam, moving them to Pennsylvania to fortify the beleaguered forces there. Putnam was charged with raising Connecticut militiamen to defend the Hudson, and for this purpose, Samuel Holden Parsons went back to Connecticut and raised an additional army of two thousand militiamen to support their beloved "Old Put." By October 9, Parsons had returned to New York and sent a letter to Trumbull begging him to send all available men to aid Putnam and stop Clinton's advance to Albany. The threat was real. Clinton had landed four thousand troops just south of Peekskill, and with Burgoyne and St. Leger on the way, Generals Samuel Holden Parsons and Israel Putnam had the task of fighting a potential thirteen-thousand-man British force with two thousand Connecticut militiamen. Clinton was moving up the Hudson, burning towns along the way. But as the fateful moment approached, stunning news came from Saratoga. Burgoyne had spread his army too thin and, outmaneuvered by the Americans, was forced to stand and fight at Saratoga. In the end, sensing a rout, he was compelled to surrender his entire army to American general Benedict Arnold. News of Burgoyne's surrender at Saratoga stopped Clinton in his tracks, and he returned to New York City. Against all odds, the Americans retained control of the Hudson, and Samuel Holden Parsons lived to fight another day.

By the end of 1777, Parsons was once again moving back and forth between Connecticut and New York as necessity dictated. On December 10, he led another raid on Long Island, landing at Hockaback (Aquebogue), about forty miles from the island's east end, and destroyed timber and materials bound for British troops in New York City. Parsons took several prisoners back with him to Connecticut. Now over forty years old and in failing health, having spent more than two years exposed to the elements and in a constant state of warfare, Parsons wrote a letter to Washington expressing his need to leave the service. It was a testament to Parsons's character that despite many entreaties to Washington and Congress, his requests were ignored, denied or met with pleas that stressed the crucial necessity of his continuing efforts. Parsons would not leave active duty for another five years.

Despite fatigue and failing health, his conviction was unwavering. In a series of archly hostile exchanges with British general Tryon in late 1777 and early 1778, Parsons's position remains clear in his defiance to British tyranny and faith in the American cause. Tryon had attacked the village of

Phillips' Manor, near the Hudson, burning private homes to the ground, attacking women and children and sending them scattering into the cold night. Camped nearby in White Plains, Parsons was outraged by Tryon's barbarity. He described Tryon's raid of November 18:

> *General Tryon sent about one hundred men under the command of Capt. Emmerick to burn some houses within about four miles of my guards, which, under cover of a dark night, he effected with circumstances of most savage barbarity, stripping the clothing from women and children and turning them almost naked into the street in a most severe night; the men were made prisoners and led with halters about their necks, with no other clothes than their shirts and breeches in triumph to the enemy's lines.*

Parsons addressed a letter to Tryon a few days later, on November 21, seeking assurances that such barbaric conduct had not been authorized by Tryon himself and, in turn, informing Tryon that the Americans had refrained from using such measures, not because they were unable or had no opportunity to do so, but because they viewed such tactics as being beyond the bounds of human decency:

> *Adding to the natural horrors of war, the most wanton destruction of private property, are acts of cruelty unknown to civilized nations, and unaccustomed in war until the servants of the King of Great Britain have convinced the impartial world, no acts of inhumanity, no stretch of despotism are too great to exercise against those they are pleased to term rebels.*

After advising Tryon, "'Tis not my inclination, Sir, to war in this manner against the inhabitants within your lines who suppose themselves with the protection of the King," Parsons makes it clear that "'tis not fear, Sir, 'tis not want of opportunity that has preserved those buildings to this time, but a sense of the injustice and savageness of such a line of conduct, has hitherto saved them and nothing but necessity will induce me to copy the example of this kind so frequently set us by your troops."

Tryon's arrogant response to Parsons two days later embraced the barbarity of His Majesty's troops and promised to double down on the terror:

> *I should, were I more in authority, burn every committee-man's house within my reach, as I deem those agents the wretched instruments of the continued*

> *calamaties of this country, and in order to soon purge this colony of them, I am willing to give twenty silver dollars for every acting committee-man who shall be delivered to the King's troops. I guess before the end of the next campaign they will be torn to pieces by their own country-men.*

Parsons's closing letter to Tryon on January 1, 1778, is a study in artfully crafted irony and insult and as lucid a statement of purpose and principle as ever penned by a Patriot. Countering Tryon's assertion that Patriots will be torn to pieces by their own countrymen, Parsons's missive informs Tryon, "[Y]ou have an undoubted right to guess again," and confidently asserts, "I shall content myself to wait til the event verifies your prediction or shows you are mistaken." Indicting the motivation behind the Tory cause, Parsons notes that "perhaps 20 silver dollars may be motives with those you employ to do great honor to your Machiavellian maxims, especially to that which advises, never to commit crimes to the halves." In a further condemnation, Parsons throws the wanton cruelty of British troops against the Americans at the Battle of Long Island in Tryon's face, saying:

> *Perhaps I might suggest with as much propriety and more truth, this unhappy event was brought about by your own party from the same motives which induced them in August 1776 to mangle the dead bodies of some of the foreign troops in almost shocking and inhumane manner, and place them in the most conspicuous parts of the roads their brethren were to pass.*

But Americans were better and held themselves to a higher standard than the British. Parsons says, "We act on a different scale and hold ourselves indispensibly bound, never to commit crimes, but to execute what's necessary for our safety uninfluenced by sordid mercenary motives." He adds: "I shall never pursue your measures for restoring peace, whether my authority should be greater or less, further than necessity shall compel me to retort the injuries the peaceable inhabitants of this country may receive from the hand of violence and oppression."

And in a resounding statement of purpose and resolve, Parsons drives home the nobility of the American cause:

> *A justifiable resistance against unwarrantable invasions of the natural and social rights of mankind, if unsuccessful, I am sensible according to the fashion of the world, will be called rebellion; but when successful, will be viewed as a noble struggle for everything important in life. Whether I am*

> *now considered as a revolted subject of the King of Great Britain, or in any other light by his subjects, is very immaterial and gives me very little concern; future ages I hope will do justice to my intentions and the present to the humanity of my conduct.*

The fight for American independence, which inspired enlightened men in both the Old and New Worlds and drew figures such as the French nobleman Lafayette and the Polish patriot Kosciusko to volunteer for battle, was given crucial support on February 6, 1778, when France recognized the United States of America as a free and sovereign nation. Most nations, for fear of confronting Britain, had refused to give the United States recognition after the Declaration of Independence on July 4, 1776. Some countries openly turned their backs on the new nation. Portugal, for example, banned all trade with the United States on July 5, 1776, and searched every American-bound vessel passing through a Portuguese port, seizing any weapons and powder found on board. But through the agency of the Marquis de Lafayette, aided by the diplomacy of Benjamin Franklin, France officially came to America's side, establishing what to this day remains as America's oldest continuous alliance. With recognition came a treaty between the two nations for mutual defense, and suddenly the scales tipped with the weight of a new element placed on the American side: the full force of the French army and navy. Soon, the fleur-de-lis would be flying on Lyme's town green at the head of French battalions and from the masts of ships off the East Coast.

Just as news of the French alliance arrived, Parsons was given command of West Point and defense of the Hudson. He was to replace Israel Putnam, now sixty years old, the ailing veteran of the French and Indian War, Pontiac's War and the Lexington alarm, hero of Bunker Hill and the Battle of Long Island. Old Put was to oversee the building of a fort at West Point, but those efforts were now in shambles. Parsons wrote, "I came to this command in most disagreeable circumstances, nothing done, everything expected and wished for and everything in confusion. I have everything to pick from perfect chaos." While he defended Old Put, his brother Freemason in the American Union Lodge, he also had the unenviable task of cleaning up his mess. Against all odds, within one month, with Kosciusko serving as engineer of the works, Parsons managed to get matters in good order and within weeks had the fort at West Point "in some state of defense," with booms and "chevaux de frise" laid across the Hudson River to ensnare British ships.

Parsons served at West Point through 1778 and 1779, making continuous excursions into Connecticut to tend to that state's defenses as well. With

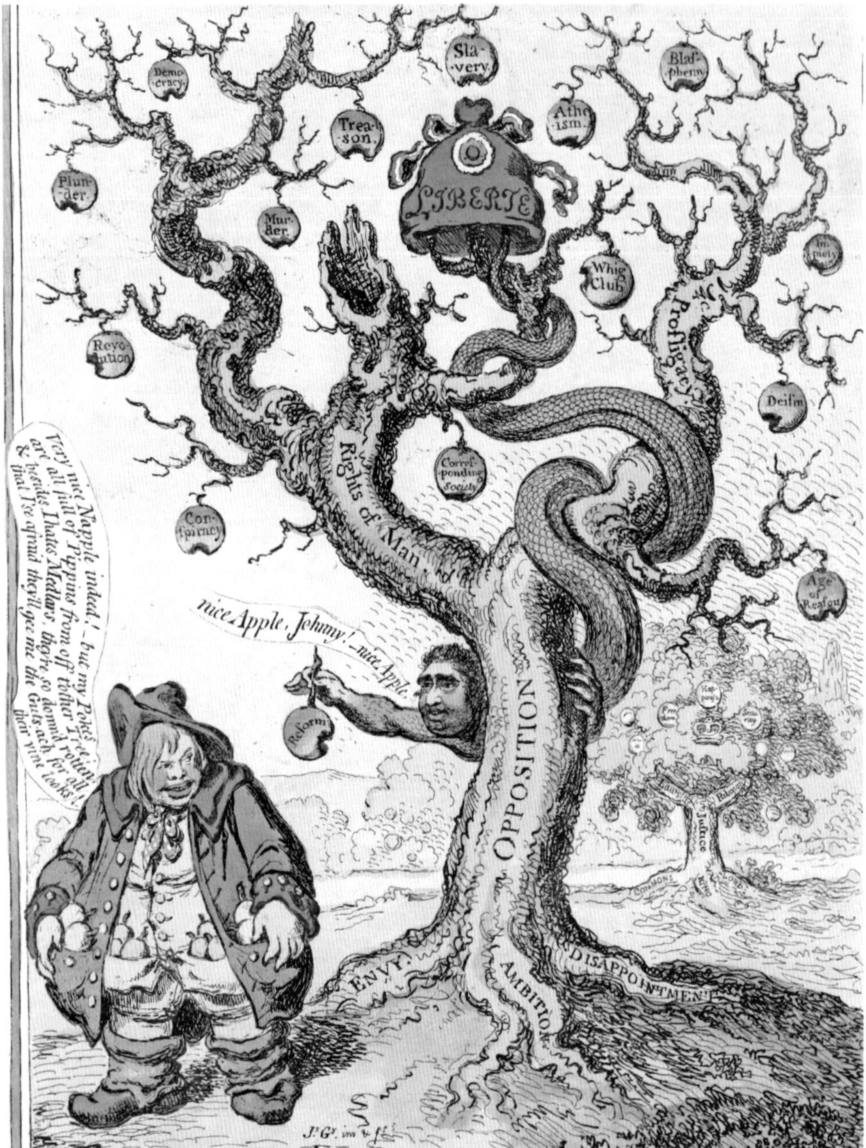

James Gillray, *The Tree of Liberty with the Devil Tempting John Bull*, circa 1778. *New York Public Library*.

the war concentrated in Philadelphia, the defense of Connecticut was not a priority. But the British, in another surprise move, evacuated the city of Philadelphia in June 1778 in order to concentrate their forces and offensive efforts in New York City and Newport. The theater of war was now coming closer to Connecticut, and the sanguine Samuel Holden Parsons, who always saw the bigger picture and was ready to sacrifice his self-interest for the sake of the larger cause, now feared for his hometown of Lyme.

The American army camped at Valley Forge was now on the move. Washington took his men to White Plains, New York, and on July 22, 1778, ordered the Marquis de Lafayette to march to Rhode Island along with Glover's and Varnum's brigades. General Lafayette was to provide support for Count d'Estaing's French fleet, which was anchored off Sandy Hook outside New York Harbor, but finding that harbor too shallow to admit his ships, d'Estaing was now on his way to confront the British navy at Newport.

Taking the shore route, Lafayette marched up the Boston Post Road and on July 28 encamped his troops on Lyme's town green. Lafayette took refreshment at Parsons's Tavern abutting the green. The tavern building had been the ancestral home of Samuel Holden Parsons, where his father, Reverend Jonathan Parsons, had raised a family with his wife, Phoebe, wrote incendiary sermons and hosted the evangelist George Whitefield. It was now a tavern run by Samuel's brother Marshfield Parsons. Marshfield, a committed Patriot and colonel in the Lyme militia, was holding the fort at Lyme, having turned the family home into a tavern that was a hotbed of revolutionary thought and action. Lyme's "tea party" had taken place near the tavern, just steps from where Lafayette's troops were now quartered.

Camped on the green under the flag of the United States of America and the French fleur-de-lis, Lafayette's troops counted Native American and black soldiers among their ranks. The marquis himself spent the evening across the street, at the home of John McCurdy, where George Washington had stayed two years prior on his journey through Lyme. The Reverend Stephen Johnson was also now back in Lyme, his congregation having refused him permission to reenlist in the army after his service at the siege of Boston. The fidelity and sympathy among these three Patriots was evident, and one can only guess as to the conversations these men had as night fell.

Completing the homecoming, General Samuel Holden Parsons had been ordered to New London in early 1779 to take command of the city and oversee its defenses, including the construction of Fort Griswold. The threat to Connecticut was no longer idle—coastal towns such as Lyme and New London were now preparing for imminent attack. The British fleet was again off Sag Harbor, with troops on board. Through his spyglass, Deputy Governor Matthew Griswold could see twenty-six British ships anchored in

Gardiner's Bay, just a few miles across the sound from his home at the mouth of the Connecticut River.

Sir Henry Clinton's troops were leaving New York City and mustering at Southampton, and more British ships were seen rounding Montauk Point. For General Samuel Holden Parsons and his uncle Matthew Griswold, the war had now come home in a very real sense.

Chapter 12

MATTHEW GRISWOLD IV

The Revolutionary Governor

Your Excellency from the enclosed papers may see in some measure the distressed situation we are in. The enemy in sight from day to day, seeming ready to wreak their vengeance upon us, the guard destitute of provision, our family store exhausted with other melancholy circumstances renders our case gloomy indeed.
—letter from Matthew Griswold to Governor Jonathan Trumbull, August 9, 1780

The deputy governor of Connecticut, Matthew Griswold IV, could see the enemy from the front steps of his home on the Long Island Sound. Just six miles to the south lay the north fork of Long Island, a Tory stronghold. Gardiner's Island and Sag Harbor, fifteen miles away, were only a short day's sail from Griswold's estate at the mouth of the Connecticut River, and British warships had been threatening since the outbreak of the war.

In July 1775, Griswold, along with several of his neighbors, exchanged fire with a boat launched from the British ship *King Fisher* anchored off the Saybrook Bar, as British sailors tried to board an American sloop that had run aground.

In the following days and months, as hostilities raged around him with battles in Boston and New York, Griswold sent entreaties to Governor Trumbull for additional resources and men to fortify the thinly guarded Connecticut coast. Though the full force of the British navy often paraded along the Lyme coast in full sight of the Griswold estate, soldiers and provisions were often needed elsewhere, and Connecticut, the Provision

State, was always prepared to impoverish itself in order to supply the needs of American soldiers in Massachusetts, New York, New Jersey and Pennsylvania.

It was known that the British were interested in blockading major ports and holding principal cities: Boston, Newport, Philadelphia and New York City. The mother country calculated that by controlling these power centers and sporadically threatening the general population elsewhere, they could wait out this foolish insurrection and bring America to heel.

But the British underestimated American resolve, and rather than making quick work of the rebels, they found themselves in a costly war that was dragging on, not for days and weeks, but for months and years. With an empire that stretched around the world, British resources were spread thin, and applications of force in the American colonies had to be used judiciously. Though Connecticut was a Patriot stronghold, supplying both the men and means for rebellion, the British had resisted a full-scale invasion that they knew would prove costly in blood and treasure but yield little in strategic value. But as the war dragged on, and the British were compelled to surrender both Boston and Philadelphia, their attention increasingly turned to this hornet's nest of revolution in Connecticut and to the leaders of the rebellion who made their home in Lyme.

Lyme's lore still rings with tales of Governor Griswold narrowly escaping British raids; his wife, Ursula, hiding him in a barrel as British soldiers searched the grounds; and young Hetty Marvin secreting him under a pile of laundry as he was escaping British pursuit while on his way to a meeting of the legislature in Hartford.

As with Reverend Stephen Johnson, Major General Samuel Holden Parsons, Colonel Samuel Selden and other Lyme Patriots, Governor Matthew Griswold, now in his sixties, was personally dedicated to the struggle. Though he was no longer actively engaged in the militia or serving in the army, Griswold and Jonathan Trumbull stood at the head of a rebel colonial government that was now a member state of a new nation, and as the war dragged on, British attention increasingly focused on these intransigent Connecticut Revolutionaries.

Connecticut's resistance to British rule was deeply rooted in the philosophy and ideals of its founders, but with the onset of war, it was also backed with force. Perhaps when ordering their navy to the shores of America, the British did not expect to be met by much opposition, as the colonists had no maritime force of their own. But in short order, Connecticut mustered one hundred private ships and, supplying them with letters of marque, enlisted them as privateers in the fight against the most powerful naval force in the

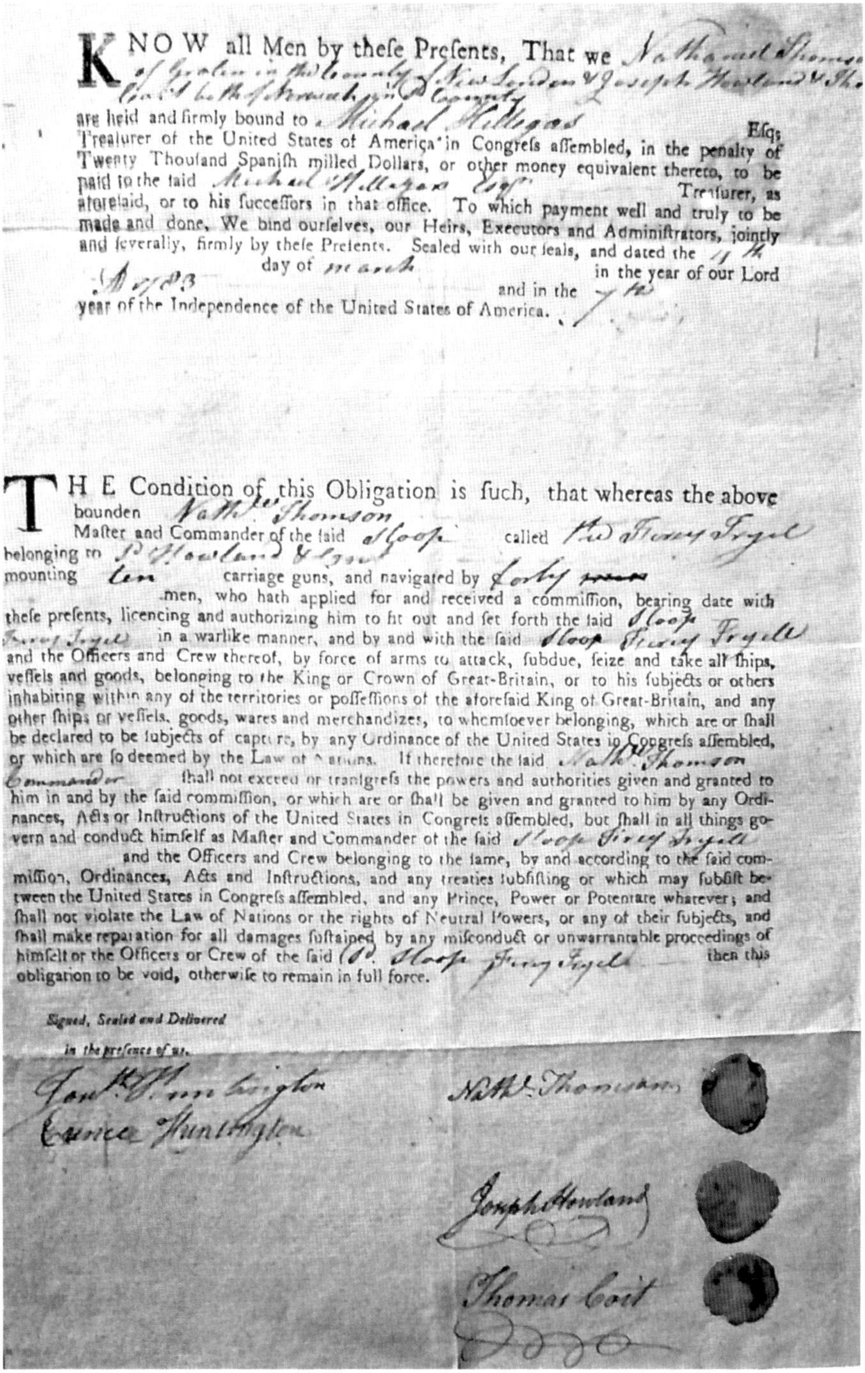

KNOW all Men by theſe Preſents, That we Nathaniel Thomson of Groton in the County of New London & Joseph Howland & Thomas Coit both of Norwich in sd County

are held and firmly bound to Michael Hillegas Eſq; Treaſurer of the United States of America in Congreſs aſſembled, in the penalty of Twenty Thouſand Spaniſh milled Dollars, or other money equivalent thereto, to be paid to the ſaid Michael Hillegas Esqr Treaſurer, as aforeſaid, or to his ſucceſſors in that office. To which payment well and truly to be made and done, We bind ourſelves, our Heirs, Executors and Adminiſtrators, jointly and ſeverally, firmly by theſe Preſents. Sealed with our ſeals, and dated the 4th day of march in the year of our Lord AD 1783 and in the 7th year of the Independence of the United States of America.

THE Condition of this Obligation is ſuch, that whereas the above bounden Nathl Thomson Maſter and Commander of the ſaid Sloop called the Firey Frygel belonging to J. Howland & Coit mounting ten carriage guns, and navigated by forty men, who hath applied for and received a commiſſion, bearing date with theſe preſents, licencing and authorizing him to fit out and ſet forth the ſaid Sloop Firey Frygel in a warlike manner, and by and with the ſaid Sloop Firey Frygel and the Officers and Crew thereof, by force of arms to attack, ſubdue, ſeize and take all ſhips, veſſels and goods, belonging to the King or Crown of Great-Britain, or to his ſubjects or others inhabiting within any of the territories or poſſeſſions of the aforeſaid King of Great-Britain, and any other ſhips or veſſels, goods, wares and merchandizes, to whomſoever belonging, which are or ſhall be declared to be ſubjects of capture, by any Ordinance of the United States in Congreſs aſſembled, or which are ſo deemed by the Law of Nations. If therefore the ſaid Nathl Thomson Commander ſhall not exceed or tranſgreſs the powers and authorities given and granted to him in and by the ſaid commiſſion, or which are or ſhall be given and granted to him by any Ordinances, Acts or Inſtructions of the United States in Congreſs aſſembled, but ſhall in all things govern and conduct himſelf as Maſter and Commander of the ſaid Sloop Firey Frygel and the Officers and Crew belonging to the ſame, by and according to the ſaid commiſſion, Ordinances, Acts and Inſtructions, and any treaties ſubſiſting or which may ſubſiſt between the United States in Congreſs aſſembled, and any Prince, Power or Potentate whatever; and ſhall not violate the Law of Nations or the rights of Neutral Powers, or any of their ſubjects, and ſhall make reparation for all damages ſuſtained by any miſconduct or unwarrantable proceedings of himſelf or the Officers or Crew of the ſaid Sd Sloop Firey Frygel then this obligation to be void, otherwiſe to remain in full force.

Signed, Sealed and Delivered in the preſence of us.

Jonth Huntington
Eunice Huntington

Nathl Thomson
Joseph Howland
Thomas Coit

Letter of marque, New London County Historical Society. *Michaelle Pearson photo.*

world. Commandeering everything from merchant vessels to sloops and whaleboats, the men of the Connecticut coast knew the Long Island Sound intimately, and no one knew the harbors and inlets of that treacherous coast known as the "Devil's Belt" better than they.

Leading merchants such as New London's Nathaniel Shaw and Lyme's John McCurdy offered their vessels up for privateering. And immediately upon the outbreak of hostilities, Connecticut shipyards set about building proper warships. The first officially commissioned warship was built in Essex, directly across the Connecticut River from Lyme, and appropriately named the *Oliver Cromwell.* Officially launched in Saybrook on June 13, 1776, the *Cromwell*, with an eighty-foot keel and twelve-foot draught, was the largest ship to cross the shallows known as Saybrook Bar at the mouth of the Connecticut River. The *Oliver Cromwell,* outfitted with twenty guns and a 180-man crew, captured several British vessels between 1777 and 1779. When the British finally captured the *Cromwell* off the coast of Sandy Hook, New Jersey, they knowingly changed the ship's name to the *Restoration*, proving that the British may have been losing the war, but they had not lost their ironic sense of humor and desire to needle the Patriots.

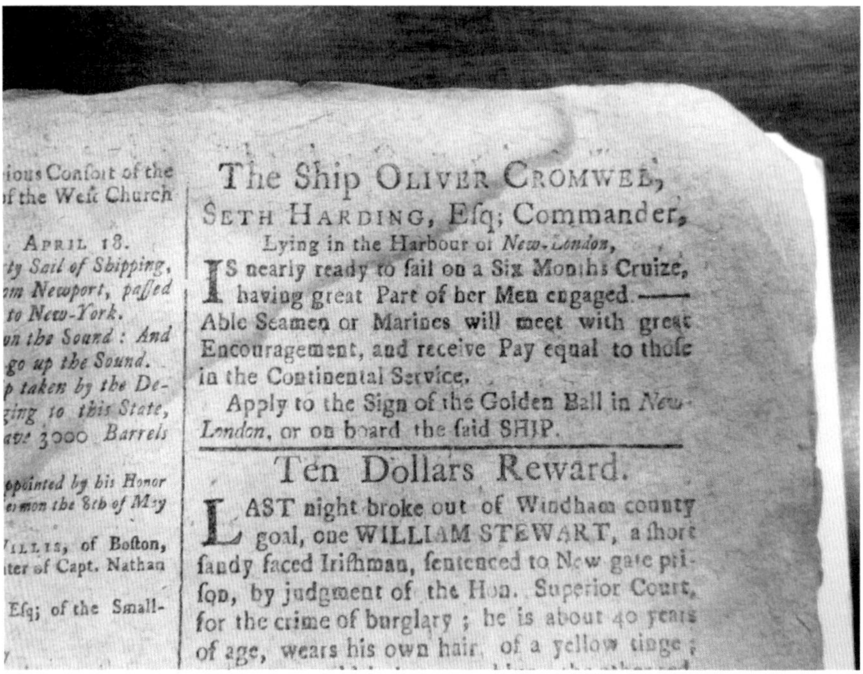

The Ship OLIVER CROMWEL,
SETH HARDING, Esq; Commander,
Lying in the Harbour of *New-London*,

IS nearly ready to sail on a Six Months Cruize, having great Part of her Men engaged.—— Able Seamen or Marines will meet with great Encouragement, and receive Pay equal to those in the Continental Service.

Apply to the Sign of the Golden Ball in *New-London*, or on board the said SHIP.

Ten Dollars Reward.

LAST night broke out of Windham county goal, one WILLIAM STEWART, a short sandy faced Irishman, sentenced to New-gate prison, by judgment of the Hon. Superior Court, for the crime of burglary; he is about 40 years of age, wears his own hair, of a yellow tinge;

Connecticut Gazette ad seeking seamen for *Oliver Cromwell*. *New London County Historical Society*.

Lyme's men, dedicated to the sea since the colony's founding, now committed themselves to its coastal defense. Among the privateers based in Lyme were the *Saucy Queen*, a six-gun schooner with a ten-man crew, commanded and bonded by Lyme's Silas Miller. Another Lyme captain, Benjamin King, captured two British ships while commanding the sloop *Washington*. The town of Lyme itself commissioned an armed boat, named *John*, outfitted with six men and one gun, captained by town resident Benjamin Conkling, who also bonded the boat along with Edward Rowland and J. Mather. The town's vessel was charged with protecting the coast.

When the British fleet anchored off Gardiner's Island in March 1779, the entire Connecticut coast prepared for attack. The twenty-six vessels in Gardiner's Bay were joined on March 29 by a fifty-gun ship and a sixty-four-gun ship rounding Montauk Point, with twenty more ships on the way from Hell Gate, at the other end of Long Island Sound. Sir Henry Clinton was also mustering British troops at Southampton in preparation for a rumored American attack on the Tory-held island. Connecticut's leaders, including Trumbull, Putnam and Parsons, had long called for such an attack, and the British had heard rumors that Parsons himself was at New London with four thousand troops planning to do just that. But, in fact, no American attack was in the works. After a tense standoff, the British fleet continued on its way, bound for New York, Newport and the West Indies. For a brief moment, Lyme's defenders breathed a sigh of relief and stood down.

Connecticut's relief was short-lived, however, as on July 5, 1779, the British attacks finally came. Parsons's nemesis, General William Tryon, landed 2,400 British troops at New Haven, looting and burning that city. On the eighth, Tryon burned Fairfield to the ground, and on the twelfth, he did the same to Norwalk. Hearing of Tryon's raids and the atrocities he was committing, Washington ordered Parsons to leave the Highlands of New York and attend to the defense of Connecticut. Arriving in New Haven on July 9, Parsons's forces were outnumbered by the British by more than than two to one. Engaging the British over the next two days, Parsons lost 5 men and had 6 wounded, while Tryon's forces, by his own report, had 20 men killed, 96 wounded and 6 missing. With each engagement, the British retreated, and by July 12, the British raids were over, though not without a final bitter exchange between Tryon and Parsons. Before the raids, on July 4, Tryon issued a proclamation to the citizens of Connecticut, which read in part:

> *The existence of a single habitation on your defenseless coast ought to be a subject of constant reproof to your ingratitude. Can the strength of*

> *your whole province cope with the force which might at any time be poured through every district in your country? You are conscious it cannot. Why, then, will you persist in a ruinous and ill-judged resistance? We hoped that you would recover from the frenzy which has distracted this unhappy country; and we believe the day to be near come when the greater part of this continent will begin to blush at their delusion. You, who lie so much in our power, afford that most striking monument of our mercy, and therefore ought to set the first example of returning to allegiance.*

Tryon had also previously addressed a letter to Parsons, on June 18: "Surely it is time for rational Americans to wish for a reunion with the parent state, and to adopt such measures as will most speedily effect it."

Parsons bided his time before issuing a mocking and contemptuous response to Tryon on September 7:

> *Surely it is time for Britons to rouse from their delusive dreams of conquest, and pursue such systems of future conduct as will save their tottering empire from total destruction.*

In the same letter, Parsons called out Tryon for being a coward and for the atrocities committed against defenseless women and children, while making it clear that his only regret was in not being able to mete out revenge face to face:

> *I should have paid an earlier attention to your polite letter of the 18th of June, had I not entertained some hope of a personal interview with you in your descents upon the defenseless towns of Connecticut, to execute your master's vengeance upon rebellious women and formidable hosts of boys and girls, who were induced by insidious proclamations to remain in those hapless places, and who, if they had been suffered to continue in the enjoyment of that peace their age and sex entitle them to expect from civilized nations, you undoubtedly supposed would prove the scourge of Britain's veteran troops, and pluck from you those laurels with which that fiery expedition so plentifully crowned you. But your sudden departure from Norwalk, and the particular attention you paid to your personal safety when at that place, and the prudent resolution you took to suffer the town of Stamford to escape the conflagration to which you had devoted Fairfield and Norwalk, prevented my wishes on that head.*

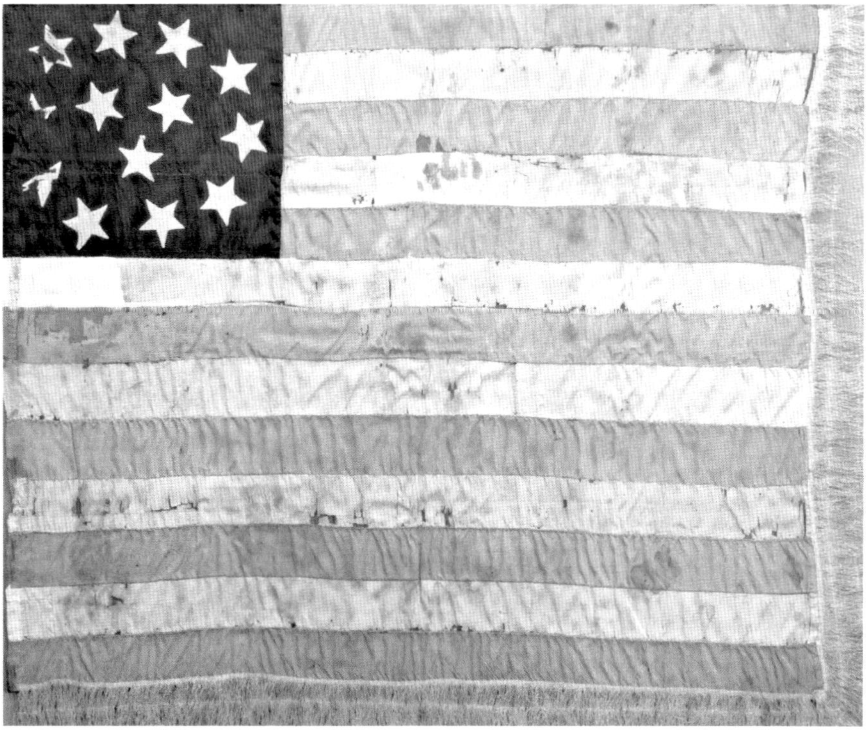

Original thirteen-star flag believed to have hung in the office of Nathaniel Shaw Jr., the naval agent for the Continental Congress and the State of Connecticut. It remains in the Shaw Mansion to this day. *New London County Historical Society*.

Despite their bluster, the British knew Connecticut was unconquerable. From the beginning, at each battle and skirmish, from Lexington to Bunker Hill on to New York and Pennsylvania, the British encountered Connecticut men prepared to fight and die for the cause of freedom. To invade their home state, particularly the eastern portion where nearly every man, woman and child was dedicated to the patriotic cause, would be sheer folly. In the southern colonies, especially South Carolina, the British enjoyed a great deal of support from Loyalist citizens. The same even held true in New York City and Long Island, where many, if not most, citizens were Tory sympathizers. It was not so in New England, especially in Connecticut. In Lyme, neither the patriotic cause nor the certainty of victory against Britain was ever in question.

In a prescient letter written by Reverend Stephen Johnson to his brother-in-law Matthew Griswold while Johnson was at camp with the Sixth Regiment in Roxbury on October 5, 1775, during the siege of Boston, Johnson stressed that he is more afraid of the enemy within than he is of the British forces:

> *Some suppose they are to make attacks on Seaports nigh us—some that they are going to Philadelphia—others to Charleston, SC—others to Quebec & C; if Burgoyne is gone to Philadelphia, I fear an insidious purpose, am more afraid of their gaining some important advantages against us by art and Corruption than by their armies; perhaps the Colonies will find it expedient to Change their Delegates often to Congress—this I believe sooner or later will be found a Measure highly important to the General Safety and welfare—& that Strict probity and incorruptibility, Join'd with some prudence and Judgement, will be safer to trust than shining abilities, Join'd with an ambitious, avaritious & designing turn of mind.*

In this letter, Johnson chillingly foretold, with his sense of ominous doings in Philadelphia featuring a character who could combine "shining abilities" with an "ambitious, avaritious & designing turn of mind," the arrival of treachery on the Connecticut coast in the guise of a native son whose name is befouled and infamous, whose character is corrupt with greed and disloyalty and whose final acts are synonymous with black-hearted treason. Perhaps only an intellectual reverend like Stephen Johnson could clearly foresee the combination of spiritual and material forces that would conspire to produce the American Judas.

Toryism was not completely unknown in Lyme, but the few who were counted among that number were swiftly dealt with and dispatched with unequivocal authority. Ironically, it was just after Cornwallis's 1781 surrender at Yorktown, but before the 1783 Treaty of Paris that signaled peace between Britain and America, that disloyal activities in Lyme turn up in the historical record. Rather than being the product of political sentiment, it appears these were the actions of men trying to make a buck after it was clear that the hostilities of the American Revolution had drawn to a close. In this period between 1781 and 1783, at a time when the United States was left in financial ruin after the war, we find men such as Lyme's Stephen Lee being caught commanding the *Fair Play*, a Lyme privateer loaded with contraband goods being smuggled from Sag Harbor in exchange for produce from Connecticut. The *Fair Play*, a six-gun schooner commissioned only that past January and carrying a crew of thirty, with the cessation of hostilities took advantage of the mercantile opportunities that presented themselves and began trading with the enemy. The *Fair Play* was captured by the privateer *Success* on April 28, 1782, commanded by Saybrook's Captain Shipman, who also captured another sloop with illegal cargo at the mouth of the Connecticut River. Such activities were less treason than crimes of opportunity.

However, a few incidents of a more political nature had occurred earlier, and the justice meted out against Tories was swift. The Lyme tea party was the first example, but another quickly followed in 1774 that served as a cautionary tale and set the tone for the sort of treatment Tories could expect

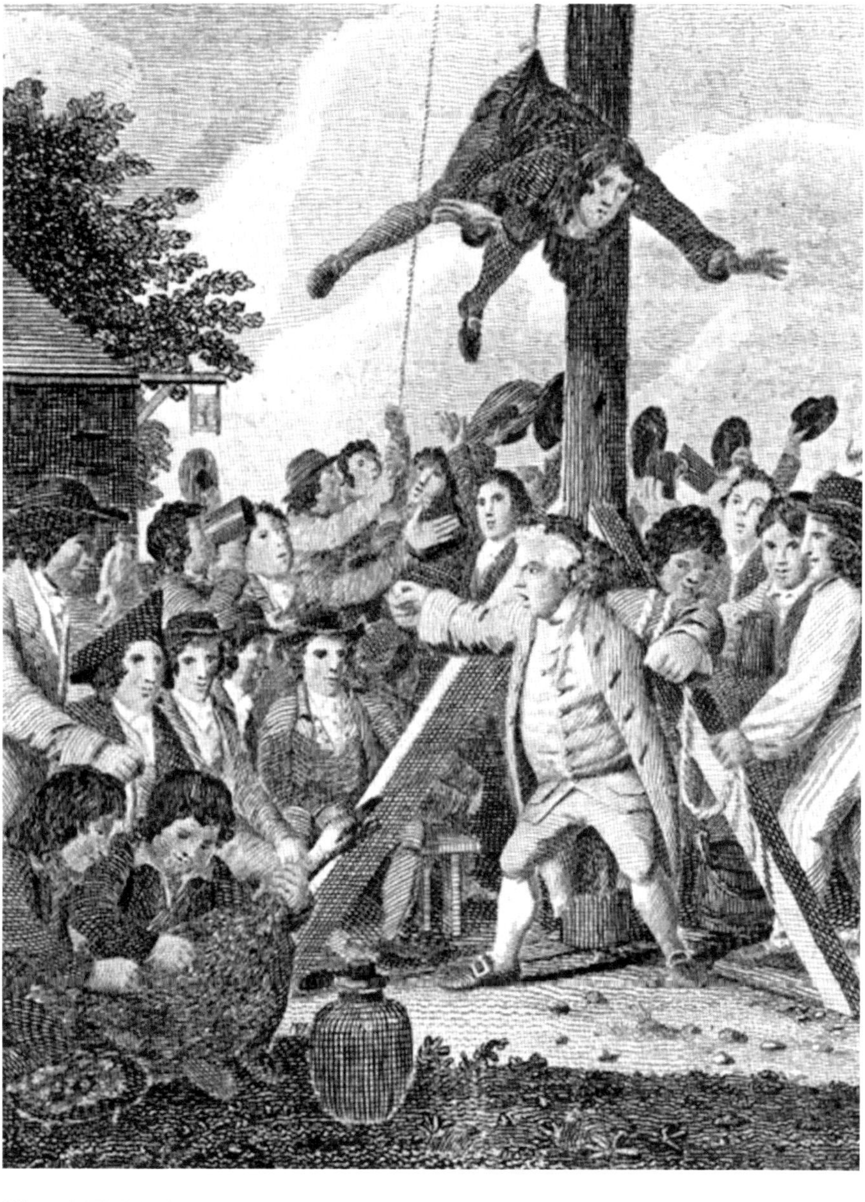

Elkanah Tisdale, *Judgment Day of Tories*. *New York Public Library*.

in eastern Connecticut. At the head of the waterfall in what is known as the Devil's Hopyard, just on the other side of Lyme's border with East Haddam, a wealthy physician and mill owner, Abner Beebe, refused to recant his British sympathies. Pressed by the Sons of Liberty to sign a loyalty oath, repudiate his statements supporting Britain's right to tax colonists and desist in his practice of drinking tea, Beebe refused. For his refusal, the Tory mill owner was beaten, stripped naked, covered in dung and paraded through the village. The Sons of Liberty then outfitted Beebe in a costume of boiling-hot tar and feathers, ransacked his home and cast his millstone down the falls, shattering it on the rocks below. Abner's brother Asa, an unrepentant Tory himself, received a matching suit of tar and feathers for good measure. The broken millstone remained at the bottom of the falls as a memento of the Revolution until 2007, when Connecticut's Department of Environmental Protection deemed it an "attractive nuisance" and removed it for storage at an undisclosed location.

Isolated incidents occurred through the subsequent years of the Revolution, proving Toryism to be the exception to Connecticut's rule. On September 29, 1777, a complaint was brought against Nathan Stark, Samuel Denison, William Angel and Jasper Champion, all of Lyme, by Lyme's Committee of Inspection and the town's selectmen, accusing Stark and his companions of being "inimical to the Liberties of this and the rest of the United States" and through "many words and actions" exhibiting "evil intentions" by passing information to the British and transporting Tories to and from Long Island.

On July 18, 1778, a complaint was brought against Roger Algers, who it was said "made in hearing of many nearby a Proclamation that he wished to God that the Hessians would come on shore and burn out the people at Black Hall and sweep the whole town of Lyme, meaning that he wished the enemie would plunder."

The most notorious of Lyme's Tories was Elisha Beckwith. On November 30, 1781, the *Connecticut Gazette* reported:

> *Last Friday under the command of Ensign Andrew Griswold, stationed at Lyme, discovered a whale boat in a fresh pond near Black Point; and suspecting it came from Long Island, they set a guard of five men over the boat; and the night after four others of the guard with Ensign Griswold, went towards the house of the noted Elisha Beckwith; one of the party named Noah Lester, advanced faster than the rest, and was challenged by Beckwith's wife, who was near the house; this alarmed ten men who were*

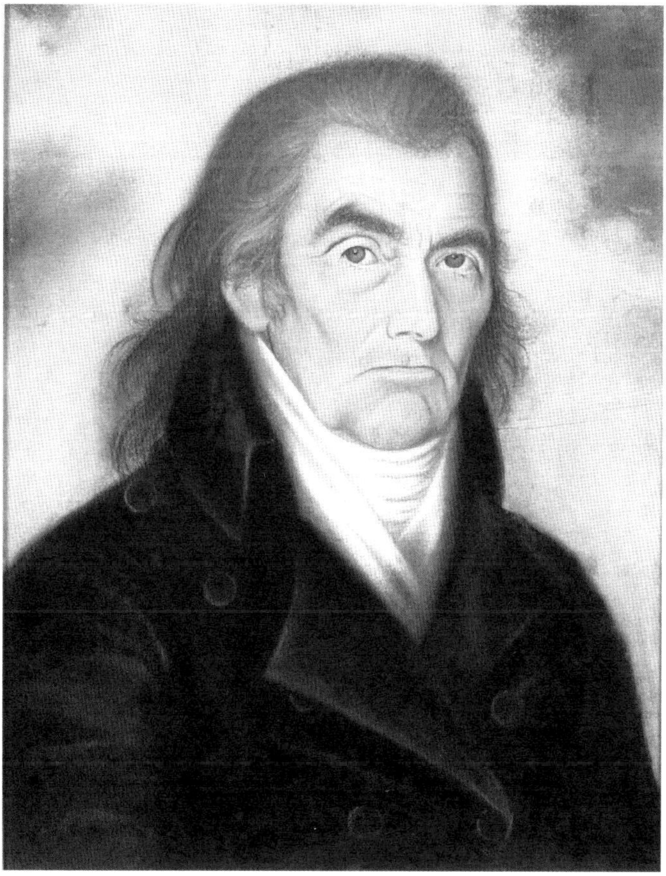

William Noyes, Esq., served as justice of New London County for thirty years. During the Revolution, his docket was filled with cases of Tories, spies and smugglers amid the more regular fare. James Martin, circa 1798. Pastel on paper. *Florence Griswold Museum purchase with contributions from Geoffrey Paul, David Dangremond, John & Werneth Noyes and Gay Myers.*

in the house, well-armed, and they immediately seized upon and made prisoner of Lester, and carried him into the house. Soon after the other four of the guard came to the house, not knowing Lester was a prisoner, and went directly in; where they discovered the ten persons in arms: a scuffle immediately ensued between them; and after some time the guard secured six of the party, among whom was Elisha Beckwith; the other four made their escape into the woods, but they all except one were taken the next day. They came in the above boat from Long Island, and were under the command of Thomas Smith, formerly of Middletown, who had a Captain's commission

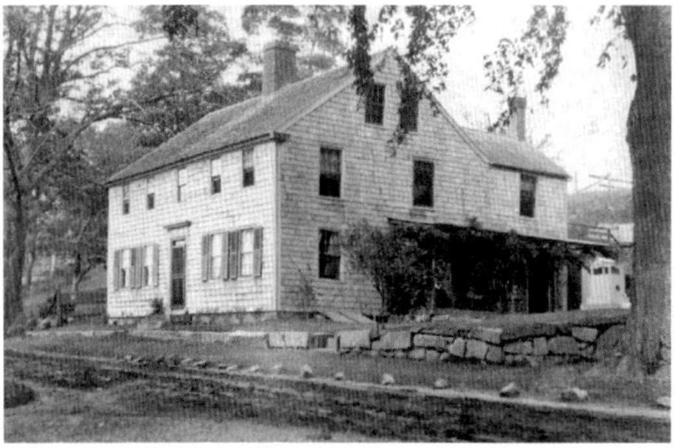

Elisha Beckwith Tory House, circa 1900. *Courtesy of the East Lyme Historical Society.*

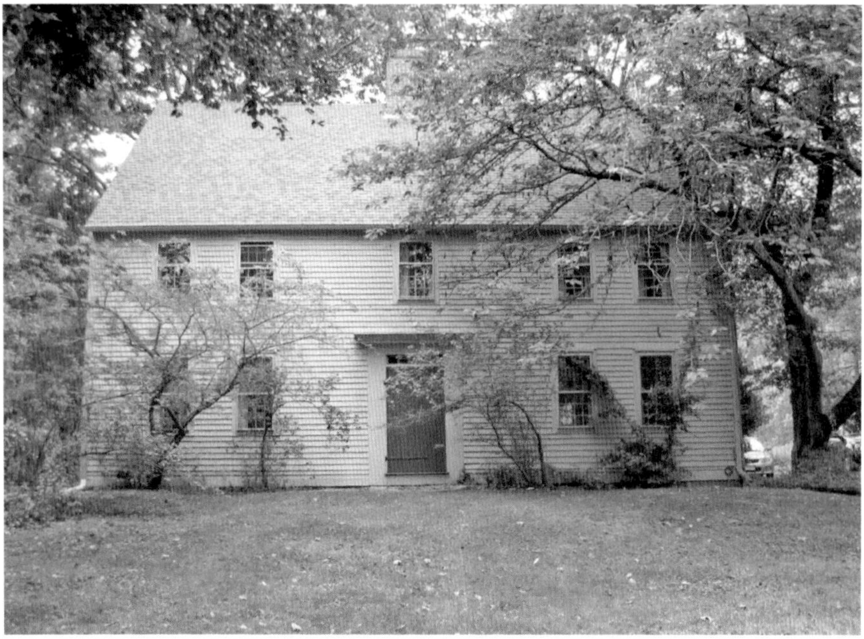

Silvanus Griswold was born in 1763, but like many young boys at the time, he helped his father and brothers "Gard our Coste—Sea Shore." Sylvanus wrote in his journal about fighting in the skirmish with the Beckwith Tories, at which Samuel and Andrew Griswold were both wounded. Silvanus Griswold House, East Lyme. *Courtesy of the East Lyme Historical Society.*

> *under the British King. Elisha Beckwith went off with the enemy the 6th Sept. last, when they made their descent on this place. The above culprits are secured in Norwich gaol.*

On January 1, 1782, Beckwith was sent to Newgate Prison in Simsbury, but at some point in the next three years, he escaped and settled in Nova Scotia.

Beckwith's crime was not of the common petty variety—a quick dollar turned trading contraband across the sound or intemperate remarks fueled by demon rum; it was of a different order. The reference in the *Connecticut Gazette* article of Beckwith going "off with the enemy the 6th Sept last" points to Beckwith's true crime: consorting with and aiding a man whose name has become synonymous with treachery—Benedict Arnold.

The only full-scale attack on Connecticut occurred late in the war, when the British cause was lost. It was a surprise attack, with its unexpected nature being not so much in timing or execution as in the person who commanded it. Benedict Arnold, revered American general, hero of Saratoga and native son of nearby Norwich, Connecticut, was now a reviled turncoat who sold himself to the British cause for a few pieces of silver. Arnold turned the full fury of his malice upon the port of New London and attacked the city, along with two forts named after the governor and deputy governor, respectively, Fort Trumbull in New London and Fort Griswold across the river in Groton. He stood upon the high hill in New London at the "Antientist Burying Ground" and watched the battle rage on the Groton side, with smoke rising from a spreading fire on the New London side that nearly reduced the entire town to ash.

Arnold had not only betrayed his country, he had also attacked his own native soil. Using his intimate knowledge of New London harbor, he burned the last bridge to human decency he possessed and destroyed the shredded vestiges of any connections he had to family, friends and associates from his life as a young Connecticut man full of promise and hope. His name now blackened, his character infamous, his cause lost, he watched as the British had their final victory in a war they would soon lose. Upon the hill in Groton, after a heroic defense, the Patriots surrendered to the British. It was said that in a final act of disgrace, Colonel Ledyard was run through with his own sword after surrendering it to the British. Whether this be fact or embellishment, it is consistent with the brutality exhibited by British soldiers against their Connecticut counterparts.

In Samuel Holden Parsons's letter to his Groton friend, fellow Son of Liberty and Ticonderoga veteran Thomas Mumford on July 20, 1779, describing Tryon's raids, he said:

> *The scandalous savage conduct of Britons in their late descents on us exceeds description.…Some of our soldiers who were killed had their skulls blown off after they were dead, and in one instance a soldier surrendered himself a prisoner after bravely defending himself a considerable time;*

> *they demanded his arms which he delivered; when he was disarmed they immediately made several thrusts with their bayonets, two of which entered him and badly wounded him.*

The brutality exhibited by the British in Groton and their abandonment of all sense of honor and gentlemanly conduct did not come as a surprise to Mumford and Parsons.

The irony of Arnold's treachery, and that of Beckwith and his confederates, was that it came so late in the struggle. Little more than a month after Arnold's attack on Groton and New London, Washington and Lafayette cornered Cornwallis in Virginia, where the British general was compelled to surrender not only his army at Yorktown but also the entire British cause in America. Cornwallis's surrender at Yorktown on October 19, 1781, signaled the end of the American Revolution. In 1783, the end of hostilities of the war between Britain and its former colonies, and the recognition of the United States of America, would be formalized with the Treaty of Paris.

Through the 1780s, America turned to rebuilding its towns and cities; restoring its agriculture, industry and shipping; and forging the document that would bind the states together under a new central authority, with a new form of representative government and a guarantee to its citizens of certain inalienable rights. By 1789, the states would ratify the new U.S. Constitution.

The prominent Revolutionaries of Lyme had somehow survived the war. John McCurdy, whose wharves, warehouses and mansion in New London were burned by Arnold, rebuilt his fortunes to the degree that, when he died on November 17, 1785, at the age of sixty-one, his estate was one of the largest in Connecticut. For his efforts in support of the Revolution, and in compensation for his losses, McCurdy had been granted lands in Ohio known as the Western Reserve. The town of Lyme, Ohio, once owned by John McCurdy, was named for his Connecticut hometown.

Reverend Stephen Johnson served out his days on Earth continuing his ministry at the First Congregational Church of Lyme, a position he held for forty years, until his death on November 8, 1786, at the age of sixty-two.

Samuel Holden Parsons, who had dedicated himself body and soul to the Revolution, was now broken in both body and spirit. His family had been left nearly destitute by Parsons's long commitment to the cause, and in 1782 he finally returned to private life, hoping to rebuild his lucrative legal practice. Settling in Middletown, he was active in the local Masonic lodge, founded the Connecticut Chapter of the Society of the Cincinnati and was again elected to the state legislature, in which he had previously served.

In 1789, he returned to the cause that had started him on the road to revolution—the western lands claimed by Connecticut under the old Susquehanna Company, now called the Western Reserve, or Northwest Territory, and dedicated as compensation to Connecticut veterans of the Revolution.

Washington appointed Parsons chief justice of the Northwest Territory, and Parsons arrived in Marietta, Ohio, in May 1788. His final words came on November 7, 1789, when he wrote to his son Enoch from the Big Beaver River in Pennsylvania, where he was surveying the Connecticut lands. Enoch had traveled with his father to the Western Reserve and was staying in Marietta. Samuel Holden Parsons died, at the age of fifty-two, while attempting to carry a man with a broken leg to a settlement for treatment. Thinking it best to transport the injured man by canoe, Parsons drowned when the canoe overturned on the rapids of the cold and swollen Beaver River. His body was not discovered until spring, and he was buried in what was to be a temporary grave along the river. Its location being lost, Parsons remains there today, at a site unmarked and unknown to posterity. Shortly after the Revolution, he was immortalized in a poem written by George Washington's aide-de-camp David Humphreys, a man who began his career in Parsons's regiment. The poem reads, in part:

> *Shall tell from whom I learnt the martial art, With what high chief I play'd my early part. With Parsons first, whose eye, with piercing ken, Reads through their hearts the characters of men.*

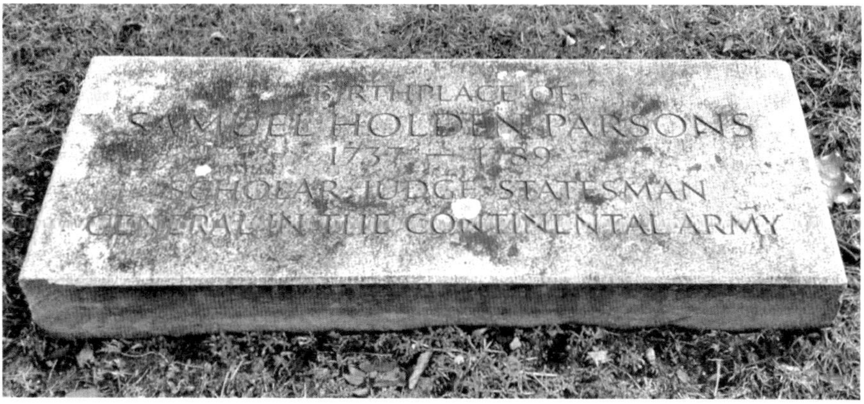

Samuel Holden Parsons marker, Old Lyme, 2016. *Michaelle Pearson photo.*

Matthew Griswold was elected governor of Connecticut in 1784, served twomyears and eventually retired to his farm at Griswold Point. He died on April 28, 1799, at the age of eighty-five. Ezra Stiles eulogized him, noting his health and clarity of mind in old age. His son, Roger Griswold, following in the family tradition, was elected governor of Connecticut on May 9, 1811. Roger was famously known for proposing the secession of New England from the Union in 1803. While one may suspect that he did so in opposition to the South's embrace of slavery, he did not, as he and his family possessed slaves. While it might be an uneasy task to parse the thoughts of the Reverends Jonathan Parsons or Stephen Johnson on the subject of slavery, Governor Matthew Griswold was unequivocal on the subject. In his essay *Remarks on Liberty and the African American Trade* penned on July 1, 1795, the governor offers a clear and direct defense of slavery. Like nearly everyone in New England, he decried the slave trade and hoped that the institution, by virtue of its own inherent contradictions, would become obsolete of its own natural accord. Indeed, by 1795, slavery had been banned in much of the Northeast. While the slave trade itself had been completely abolished, the ownership of slaves already in one's possession was still legal in Connecticut. In 1784, Connecticut passed legislation calling for the gradual emancipation of slaves: children of slaves were to become free at twenty-five, and soon thereafter the age was lowered to twenty-one.

In 1788, Connecticut banned the trade and importation of slaves altogether. But the continued ownership of slaves remained legal. Griswold's defense of slavery in 1795—a time when slavery was already seen as a retrograde institution and many slave owners had either already voluntarily freed their slaves or provided for their freedom in their wills—rested on the notion of property rights. It was this notion—the sanctity of private property—that divided the freedom-loving Patriots of New England on the question of freedom itself. Griswold's compromise in 1795 was this: slaves were neither to be bought or sold, but the ones already held as property need not be freed. He wrote:

> *By a Sovereign Act to set them all free at one blow and Dissolve the Legal Right of the Masters to their Service, which the Masters Purchased with their own money, under the Sanction of the Law, would be rather using the Law as a snare to deceive the people.*

Grounding his opposition to abolition in this legalese, and asserting the primacy of the property rights of slaveholders over the human rights of their servants, Griswold goes on:

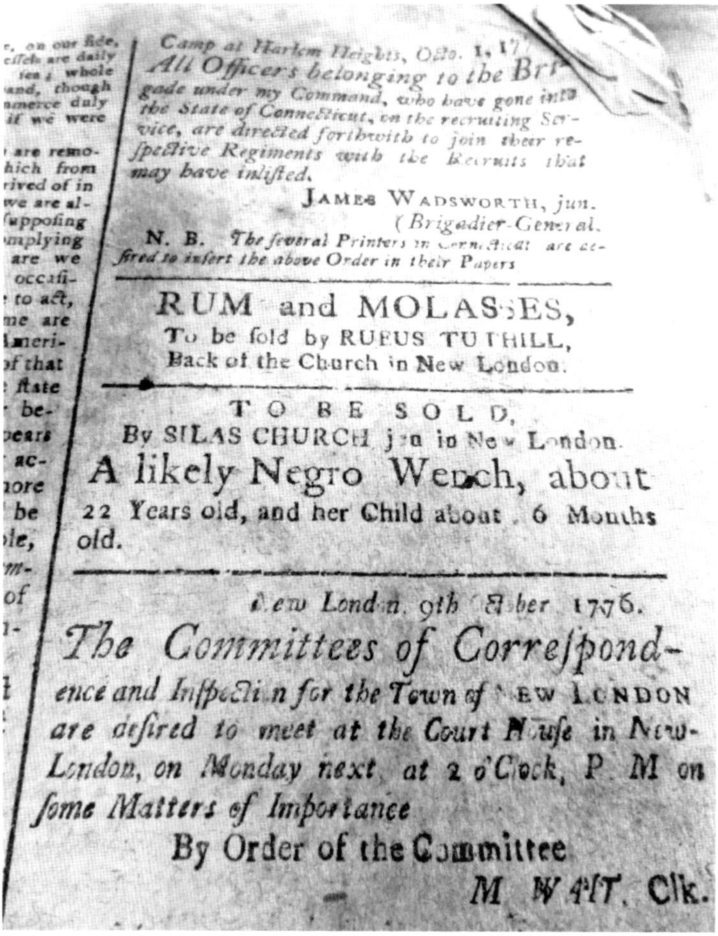

Camp at Harlem Heights, Octo. 1, 17

All Officers belonging to the Brigade under my Command, who have gone into the State of Connecticut, on the recruiting Service, are directed forthwith to join their respective Regiments with the Recruits that may have inlisted.

JAMES WADSWORTH, jun.
(Brigadier-General.

N. B. The several Printers in Connecticut are desired to insert the above Order in their Papers

RUM and MOLASSES,
To be sold by RUFUS TUTHILL,
Back of the Church in New London.

TO BE SOLD,
By SILAS CHURCH jun in New London.
A likely Negro Wench, about 22 Years old, and her Child about 6 Months old.

New London, 9th 8ber 1776.

The Committees of Correspondence and Inspection for the Town of NEW LONDON are desired to meet at the Court House in New-London, on Monday next, at 2 o'Clock, P. M on some Matters of Importance

By Order of the Committee
M WAIT, Clk.

Connecticut Gazette advertisements for rum to be sold behind the church, a slave for sale and a meeting notice of the New London Committee of Correspondence, 1776. *New London County Historical Society.*

The master ought to learn his servant to Read and understand the Bible.... Supply him with the necessities of life in a Reasonable Manner, in sickness and health, speak kindly to him, Encourage him in his Business, give him the Praise when he does well, Chear his spirits, but not with Fondness or Familiarity; let him know his proper distance.

Thus defining a paternalistic, yet benevolent, code of conduct that is careful to maintain the distinctions of social order, Griswold drives his point home and asserts that the manumission of slaves is a threat to the republic itself:

> *I am sensible that the idea of being commanded by the will of another is Disagreeable to the feelings of the Humane mind under its Present Depravity: but that Impression is merely Imaginary....Those Servants in Connecticut under the care and Guardianship of kind masters, and contented where they are well Provided for, without any care or anxiety of their own, are some of the Happiest People in the State....but such is the Misery of the fallen race that many of them cannot bear Prosperity: Preferment, Wealth, Respect, and kindness inflames their Pride and Haughtiness....I wish that every person was Posses'd of the Virtue, Industry, and Prudence that Qualifies a Person for Freedom, and Proper Measures were taken to make all free: But to set such free as ought to be Restrain'd wou'd tend to sap the foundation of Civil Government.*

And, so, the fissure that would undermine the nation in the next century became clear.

In Revolutionary America, the surest path to freedom for a slave was service in the army. While some were kept in segregated units, other regiments, such as those of Samuel Holden Parsons, were integrated. In his ranks, we find Lyme's Peter Freeman, an African American soldier who fought alongside his white brethren and also in dedicated black regiments, from 1778 until his discharge in 1780. Another black soldier from Lyme, Caesar Goldsmith, fought in the same unit as Lyme's John Lay, a white soldier. In the writings of Samuel Holden Parsons, unlike those of his father, Jonathan, or his chaplain Reverend Johnson, the word slavery does not appear. As one of the most eloquent writers on the subject of liberty, he falls silent on the question of slavery. Still, his actions speak where his words do not, and the service of African American soldiers from Lyme in the ranks of the Continental army during the Revolution, fighting in integrated units, some alongside their former masters, speaks volumes to the future course that the cause of freedom would take in the new nation in general and New England in particular. In the Lyme land records, we find that the slave Peter Freeman was freed by his master, Samuel Ely, on February 13, 1781. It is interesting to note that the epitaph on the grave of Samuel's father, William Ely, who died in 1758, reads, "He was the first among us to free his slaves." It was a matter of pride to be marked on a tombstone.

The names and final resting places of the more than one hundred men of Lyme who served in the Revolutionary War are known, and a walk through the burying grounds of Old Lyme, East Lyme, Lyme and Salem rewards the visitor with a palpable connection to the past.

In these evocative, little-changed landscapes of venerable oaks, maples, beeches and elms, with hand-carved stones of local slate, sandstone and

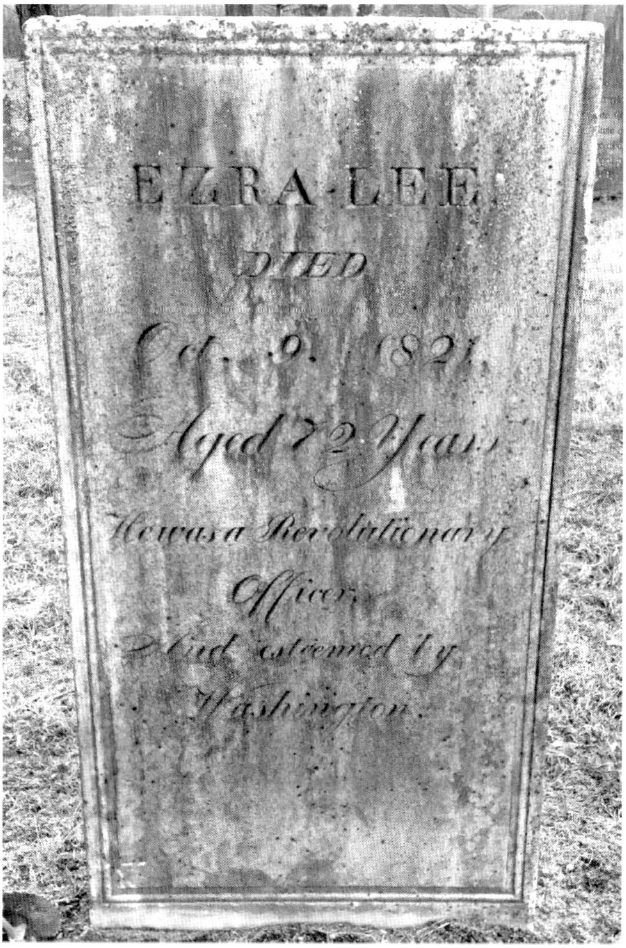

Ezra Lee's gravestone at the Duck River Cemetery in Old Lyme reads, "He was a Revolutionary Officer, And esteemed by Washington." *Michaelle Pearson photo.*

granite memorializing their lives, the veterans of the American Revolution are still remembered, with flags placed on their graves each year. Walking from stone to stone, one gets a sense of the magnitude of the struggle and the dedication of these soldiers to the cause of liberty.

In Old Lyme's Duck River, we find Governor Matthew Griswold, Reverend Stephen Johnson, John McCurdy, Marshfield Parsons and *Turtle* pilot Ezra Lee all buried in close proximity to one another. In the Old Stone Church Burial Ground in today's East Lyme, we find many who answered the alarm at Lexington and served in Parsons's and Storrs's regiments.

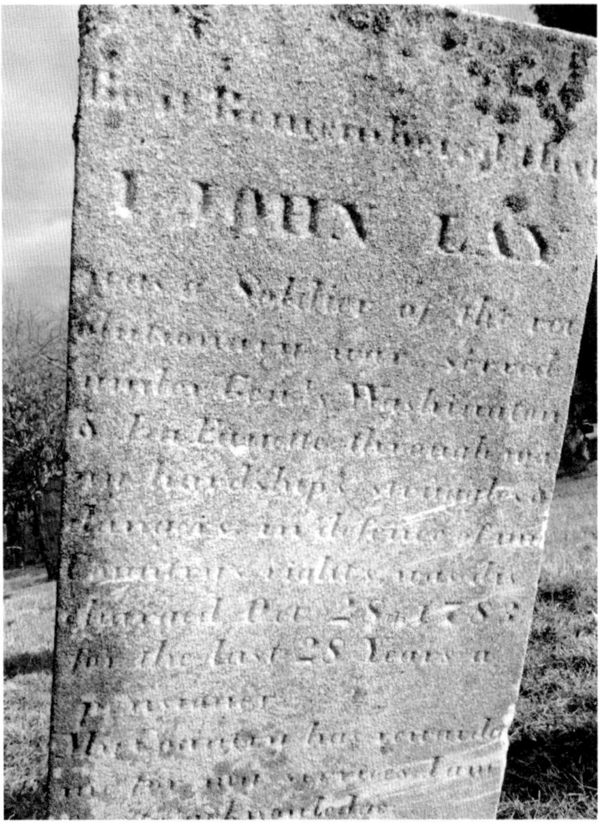

John Lay gravestone, Old Lyme, 2016. *Michaelle Pearson photo.*

Scores of others are found in small graveyards throughout the Lymes, and their names are also recorded in books, such as the Connecticut Military Record. Each name within has a story to tell. Sometimes we can find the stories told to us, written on the stones of the burying ground. In Old Lyme's Meeting House Hill Cemetery, we find the epitaph of John Lay, a man who was deserving of the nation's gratitude and who, in turn, expresses his own gratitude to the nation in return:

> *Be it Remembered that I, John Lay was a Soldier of the Revolutionary War, served under Gen's Washington & La Fayette, through many hardships, struggles, dangers in defence of my Country's rights, was discharged Oct 28th 1783 for the last 28 Years a pensioner. My Country has rewarded me for my services, I am free to acknowledge: Died June 20 1846 & 89 Yr's 7 mon's*

Chapter 13

The Tree of Liberty

I congratulate you my dear sister upon your elevation to the dignified and enviable station of housekeeper and head of the family. I have no doubt but you will do great honor to yourself, and our country, and family, and merit a continuance of the good opinion and admiration of the "Nation's Guest," and the redoubtable Alderman Doughty and all the rest of the "Great gods and little fishes." In fact, I can see you now, in my mind's eye, reflected in that brilliant teapot with cap akimbo and smirk irresistible, looking down all opposition and pouring out the hottest of bohea in the most graceful and fascinating manner.

I am gratified to hear that you want nothing to complete your happiness but a beau, and that difficulty I shall obviate as soon as the General returns by sending him and all his suite—so you must pin up your curls, lace tight, practice attitudes—smiling and pouring out coffee & eat chalk and vinegar until he comes along. I trust to luck for the rest—Mrs. Rowland who arrived a few days since tells me that you have so disguised the old mansion to correspond with other matters that even The General would hardly recognize it as the "hospitable roof of R. McCurdy, Esqr" where he once did himself the honor to take breakfast.

Robert H. McCurdy in New York, to his sister Sarah in Lyme, June 4, 1824

In the nearly half century since the Declaration of Independence, there were few events that galvanized the new nation and captured the imagination of its citizens as the prospect of a visit from the Marquis de Lafayette in 1824. Perhaps only the inauguration of his dear friend George Washington could compare in filling the nation's bosom with pride and

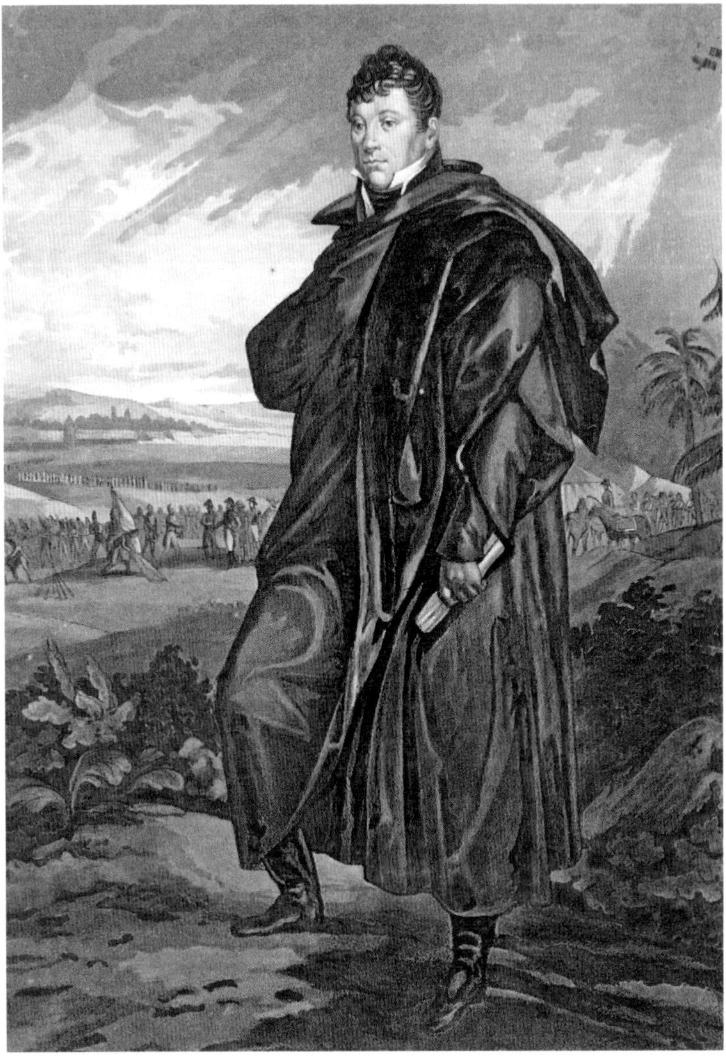

Lafayette was received joyfully by a grateful nation in 1824–25. "The Nation's Guest" breakfasted in Lyme at the McCurdy mansion en route to New London. Matthew Harris Jouett, 1825. *New York Public Library.*

unifying its citizens as the visit of General Lafayette, the "Nation's Guest," who over the course of the next year toured the entire nation to the adulation of all its men, women and children.

One of the last surviving heroes of the American Revolution, Lafayette was fêted, honored, breakfasted, banqueted, paraded, toasted and canonized as a secular saint as he made his way from town to town. Everyone clamored to see him. Every city, village and hamlet vied for a visit, each one planning a more elaborate celebration in his honor than the next. Memorial arches were built, ballrooms festooned with bunting and parade routes lined with children raining flower petals upon the man known as the "Hero of Two Worlds."

As a teenager, Lafayette had dedicated himself and his treasure to the cause of American liberty. He was first inflamed by Enlightenment ideals and the cause of freedom in the military Masonic lodges of France, and when the American colonists took up arms against France's archenemy, England, in 1776, the young nobleman said, "As soon as I heard of American Independence, my heart was enlisted." He outfitted a ship and sailed to America, offering to fight for no compensation and to pay for his expenses out of pocket. At the age of nineteen, he was made a major general in the Continental army, serving and fighting with distinction from Brandywine to Rhode Island and at Washington's side in Yorktown for Cornwallis's surrender.

Returning to his native France a hero, he advocated for universal freedom, authored *The Declaration of the Rights of Man and of the Citizen* and promoted the ideas that would spark the French Revolution. Though he was one of the noble voices of the French Revolution from its inception, events soon overtook him, and his call for moderation was seen as treason by monarchists and revolutionaries alike.

As the Reign of Terror swept France, culminating in the execution of King Louis XVI and his wife, Marie Antoinette, Lafayette faced rebellions among the Jacobites in the ranks of the National Guard he commanded and was forced to flee France. His wife, Adrienne, barely escaped the guillotine, and Lafayette himself suffered a harsh imprisonment by Austrian authorities at Olmutz who saw him as a dangerous revolutionary. Having survived these ordeals, the youngest American general, and one of the last surviving officers of the Revolutionary War, was now returning to the land he loved and for which he had fought. That land, now a free and prosperous nation, dearly loved him in return.

The festivities that greeted the Marquis de Lafayette upon his arrival in New York City were unlike any that had been seen in the young nation's history. Thirty thousand people greeted him at the Battery, another fifty thousand watched the parade as he made his way up Broadway to city hall and a massive banquet was held in his honor at Castle Garden. The effect upon the city and, over the course of the next year, upon an entire nation was electrifying.

Walt Whitman was a young child when Lafayette picked him up and kissed him at a parade in Brooklyn. It was an event Whitman never

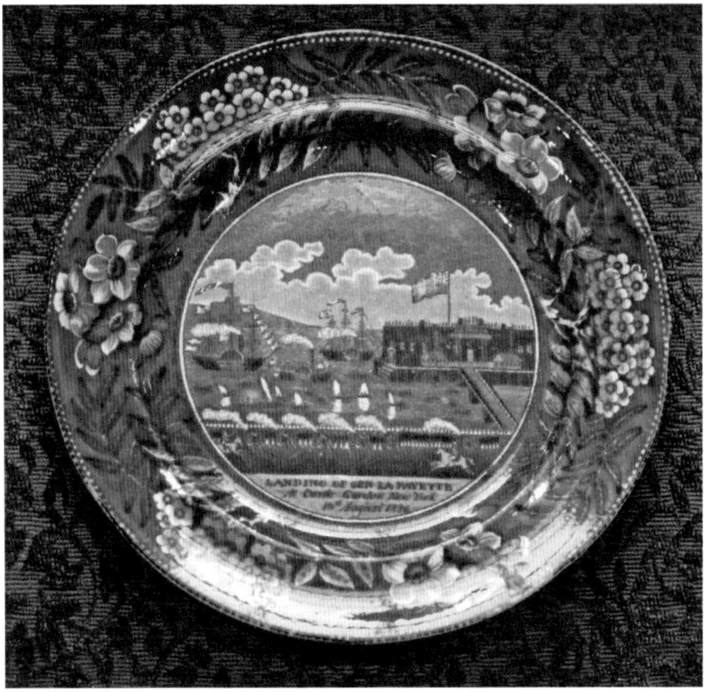
LANDING OF GEN LA FAYETTE

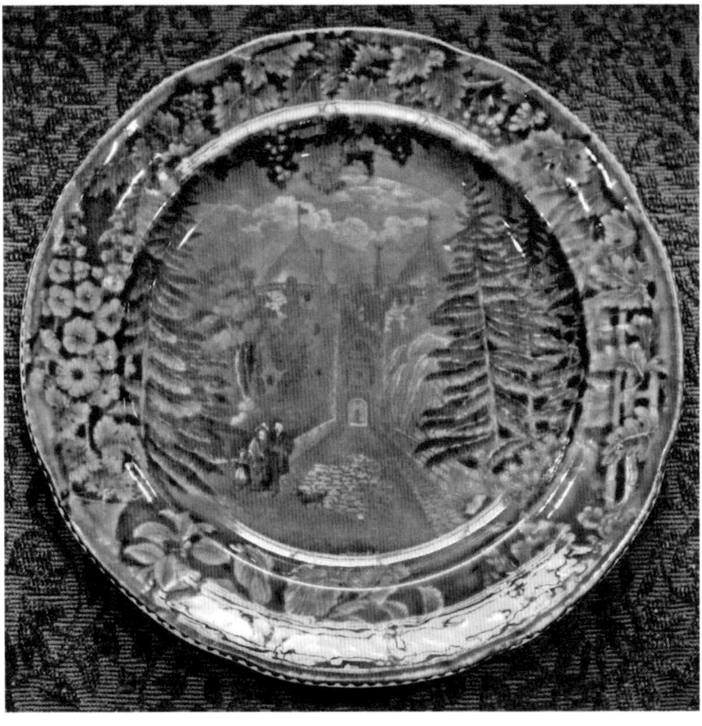

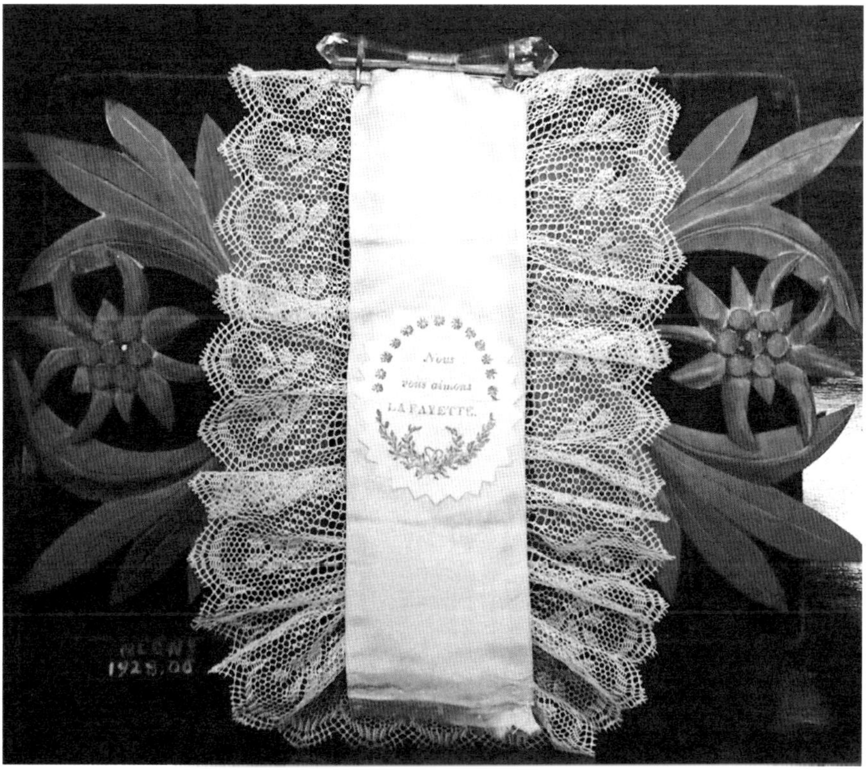

Lafayette souvenir badge, circa 1824. *New London County Historical Society.*

Opposite: All manner of souvenirs were produced for Lafayette's visit in 1824–25, from simple ribbons to full sets of Staffordshire ware. These Enoch Wood plates, *The Landing of Lafayette* and *LaGrange, Residence of the Marquis Lafayette*, are among those once owned by the McCurdy family. *Florence Griswold Museum; gift of the Phoebe Griffin Noyes–Old Lyme Library, from the Evelyn MacCurdy Salisbury Ceramics Collection.*

forgot and provided a visceral connection for America's great bard to the very foundation of the republic. Though Lafayette did not make an immortal poet of all he blessed on his journey, the impression he left upon the national character was indelible and continued to reverberate for generations. His arrival was a singular event that bound the nation together and helped forge a unified national identity. In a sense, Lafayette was a mirror in which the young nation could finally see its own reflection and reflect upon its own image.

After a week in New York, Lafayette made his way to Boston to visit the elder statesman of Quincy, President John Adams. Traveling on the Post Road along the Connecticut coast, Lafayette's carriage was greeted with cheering throngs by day and solemn torchlight vigils by night. As he neared

Lyme, a reporter said he'd overheard Lafayette's carriage driver talking to his horse: "Behave pretty, now Charley, behave pretty, Charley—you are going to carry the greatest man in the world." From far and wide across the state, farmhand, merchant, cleric, servant, selectman and Masonic grand master came to pay their respects to the man Connecticut residents, in their unique accent, called "The Markis."

Robert McCurdy's letter to his sister Sarah detailing preparations for Lafayette's visit to the McCurdy home in Lyme was written over two months before the general's ship *Cadmus* arrived at New York Harbor on August 15, 1824. While much of Lafayette's itinerary was improvised after he arrived in America, it was clear that this return to the McCurdy mansion was firmly fixed even before Lafayette left France—a sign of the great esteem Lafayette held for the McCurdy family. The important revolutionary city of New London, for example, didn't know for sure if Lafayette would visit until August 18, just days before his arrival. Robert McCurdy, on the other hand, was writing to his sister in June of Lafayette's planned visit to their ancestral home, indicating that not only did Lafayette view a stop in Lyme as a must, but also that McCurdy, a prominent merchant of New York City, was well connected with the marquis and in contact with him while he was still in France. He was thus able to write to his sister with certainty, well in advance, that the Nation's Guest would be paying them a visit.

Lafayette spent the night of August 21 in Saybrook, a town that will go down in history as the only one on the yearlong tour that would actually charge the Hero of Two Worlds for a meal. The marquis graciously paid his tab at the Pratt Tavern without blinking an eye. Across the river in Lyme, the good general would, of course, as in the rest of the nation, not have to spend a dime. Lafayette arrived on Lyme's shores on the morning of August 22 and was received in the sunny East Room of the McCurdy manse by the eighteen-year-old lady of the house, whom Lafayette would many years hence call the "beautiful Miss McCurdy." Sarah was described as having blue eyes, with a "complexion like snow, yet with rosy tints"; she had, in Evelyn McCurdy's words, "inherited the quickness of perception and bright wit of her family." Her charms were not lost on the marquis, and the morning he spent in the McCurdy home remained a cherished memory.

After his visit to the McCurdys, the general and his entourage set out on the newly built Lyme–New London Turnpike, following the path of the old Country Road, toward New London. Along the way, he was greeted by a delegation of that town's citizens, and after another breakfast at the Caulkins Tavern at the headwaters of the Niantic, he was met by Moses Warren, a

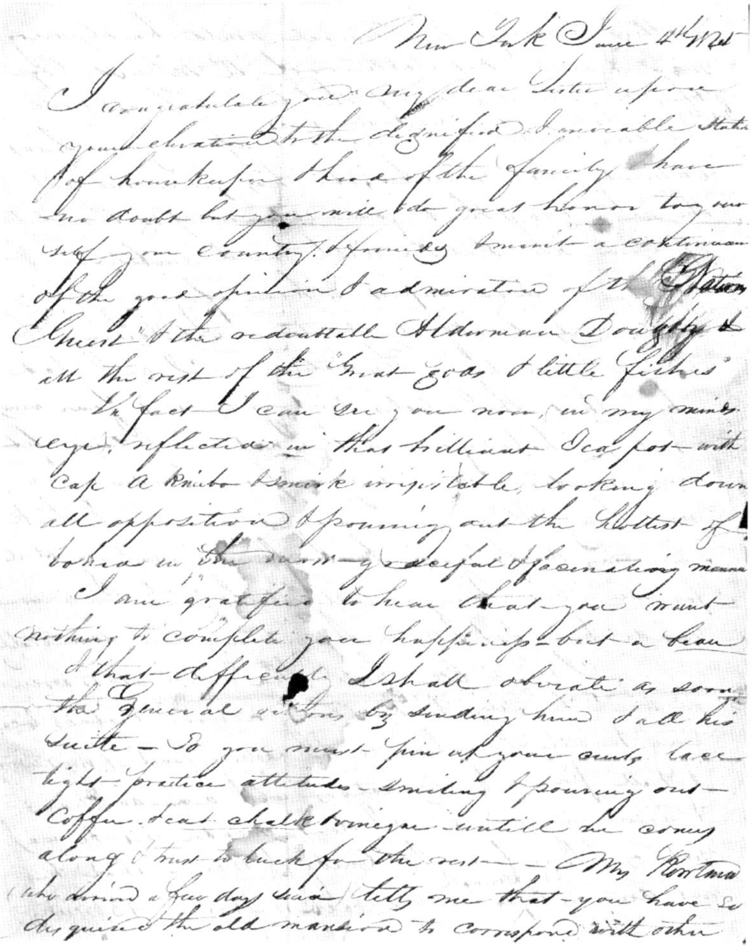

New York June 4th 1825

I congratulate you my dear Sister upon your elevation to the dignified & enviable State of housekeeper & head of the family. I have no doubt but you will do great honor to your self, your country & family & merit a continuance of the good opinion & admiration of the Station Guest & the redoubtable Alderman Doughty & all the rest of the "Great goes & little fishes."

In fact I can see you now, in my minds eye, reflected in that brilliant tea pot—with cap a kimbo & smirk irresistable, looking down all opposition & pouring out the Hottest of bohea in the most graceful & fascinating manner. I am gratified to hear that you want nothing to complete your happiness but a beau & that difficulty I shall obviate as soon [as] the General returns by sending him & all his suite—So you must pin up your curls, lace tight, practice attitudes, smiling & pouring out coffee & eat chalk & vinegar untill he comes along & trust to luck for the rest—My Boatman (who dined a few days since) tells me that you have so disguised the old mansion to correspond with other

Letter from Robert H. McCurdy in New York to his sister Sarah in Lyme, mentioning Lafayette's visit. *Lyme Historical Society Archives, Florence Griswold Museum.*

past master of Lyme's Pythagoras Lodge and a Revolutionary War veteran. Lafayette proceeded to New London for a reception at the Shaw Mansion. It was there that Lafayette entered the bedroom where Washington stayed during the early days of the Revolution, and the marquis knelt at the bedside in silent prayer and remembrance of the nation's founding father.

A recurring theme in the accounts of Lafayette's journey is the acuity of his memory. Traveling along the highways and byways, Lafayette always remembered those who had served with him in the war, even after the endless toasts of a Masonic banquet. As he stepped out of his carriage in a sleep-deprived state at some way station between here and there, a marginal figure might emerge from the crowd, hand extended, purporting to know or have personally served with the great marquis. If this were true, Lafayette would remember, and shaking off the haze of years and spirited toasts to American democracy at that night's celebration, Lafayette would not only produce the name of the grizzled veteran but also call up an anecdote or moment that would be proof of the man's caliber. It was often noted that Lafayette paid special attention to the black veterans who approached him, as many had served nobly in his ranks.

When Lafayette first stayed at John McCurdy's home in 1778, with his troops quartered across the street on Lyme's town green, it was noted that those serving under the stars and stripes of the new nation and the fleur-de-lis of its oldest ally were a diverse array of men high born and low, Americans and Frenchmen, Yankees and Native Americans, freemen and slaves. This "motley crew" was one of the most disciplined, well dressed and impressive in the American army. Under the command of the elegant democrat Lafayette, they were the new face of the new nation—all men equal under the sun, judged by the quality of their character and assessed by their conduct and demeanor. But the home in which Lafayette spent the night was tended to by slaves, as McCurdy himself was a slave owner. We can't know what conversation transpired between John McCurdy and Lafayette that day, but we do know that when Lafayette returned in 1824, the McCurdy family no longer held slaves, and indeed, many of Lyme's families had freed their slaves quickly after the Revolution. In that sense, Lafayette was able to witness two victories in Lyme upon his return: the prosperity of a new nation and the ending of slavery, an institution that he saw as being antithetical to American values.

Perhaps Lafayette's tour from 1824 to 1825 was the first spark of national unity at a time when the old Federalist order was fading and the founders were passing away. The first half century of freedom saw fierce battles over states' rights, federal power and international entanglements. In this period, even the notion of New England's secession from the Union was proposed and advanced by Matthew Griswold's son Roger Griswold, a Connecticut representative to the U.S. Congress and future governor himself. But as the nineteenth century matured, the men and women of Lyme, whether they were elected leaders or ordinary citizens, were united in support of abolition. When the first shots were fired by Confederate troops, the people of Lyme sprang to the defense of their country with unanimity of purpose, just as they had when the first shots were fired in Lexington eighty-six years earlier. The founding families of Lyme served with as much distinction in the Civil

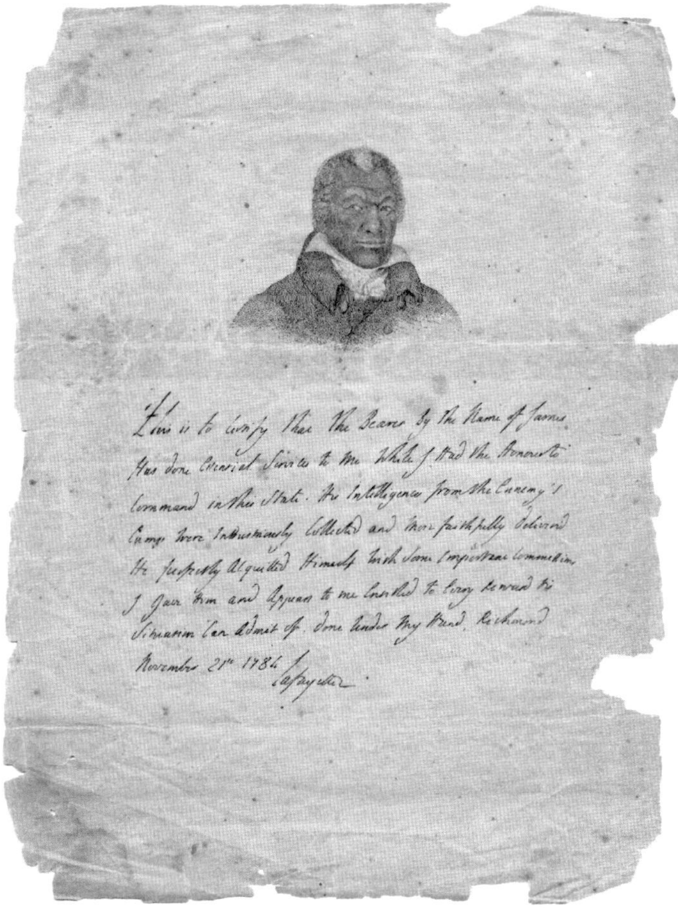

This is to certify that the Bearer by the Name of James Has done Essential Services to me While I Had the Honour to Command in this State. His Intelligences from the Enemy's Camp were Industriously Collected and more faithfully Delivered He perfectly Acquitted Himself with Some Important Commissions I Gave him and Appears to me Entitled to every Reward his Situation Can Admit of. Done under my Hand, Richmond November 21st 1784

Lafayette

Lafayette's testimonial for James Armistead, an African American slave who joined his regiment as a spy. "His intelligences from the enemy were industriously collected and most faithfully delivered.…He appears to me entitled to every reward." James was granted his freedom in 1787 and took the surname Lafayette in gratitude. *New York Public Library.*

War in defense of the Union as they had in the Revolutionary War in defense of American liberty.

No one would know better than Lafayette that the road to freedom is not direct. Sometimes the path is lost in the bramble, just as the streams of liberty that road traces may disappear underground or become obstructed by fallen limbs or the works of man and, in their neglected state, form pestilential swamps. But those spirited waters eventually find their level, making their way toward the sea and, in so doing, nourishing the land. And in traveling

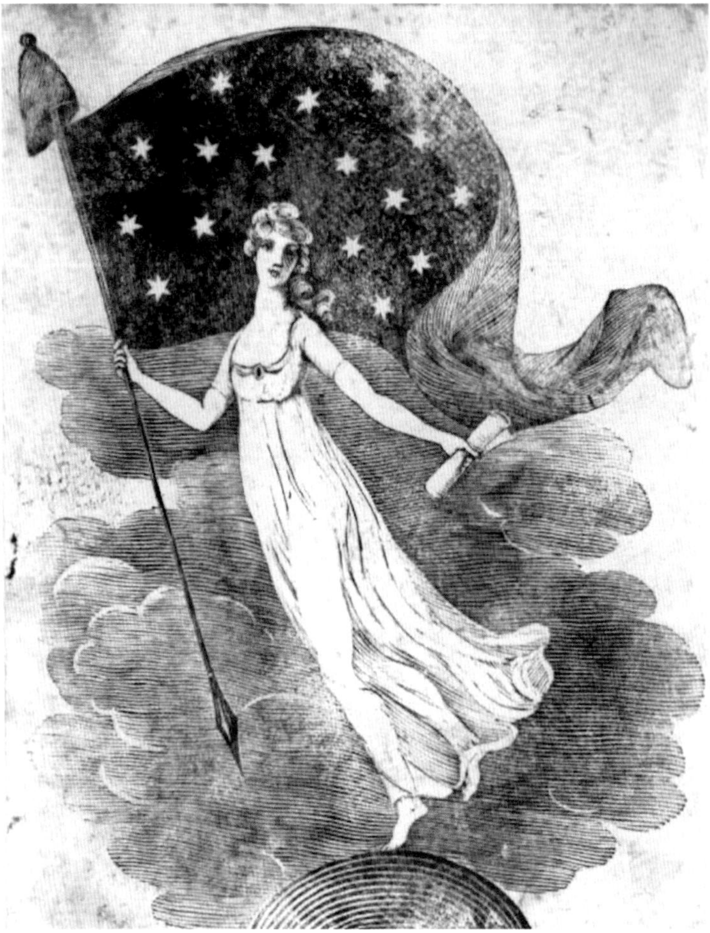

Alexander Anderson, *Allegory of Liberty*. *New York Public Library*.

down freedom's road, the Old Post Road, and entering the streamside burying ground that hosts the graves of Lyme's founders, one can point to any venerable oak or some other specimen of antiquity and dub it the Tree of Liberty and see that tree partaking of those clear, free-flowing waters. And while the leaders and boughs of the Tree of Liberty are often twisted, gnarled and deformed, the tree itself—rooted firmly in the bones of the martyrs and Patriots buried beneath it—is sound and strong. And looking up, one can see that its shoots and branches are ever growing, ever aspiring and still ever tending toward the light.

Bibliography

Primary Source Manuscripts

Elizabeth Plimpton Papers. Lyme Local History Archives/Lyme Public Hall Association, Inc.

Griswold Family Papers. Wolcott G. Lane Collection. Jonathan Gillet Collection. Lyme Historical Society/Florence Griswold Museum.

Parsons, Jonathan. *Notebook of Handwritten Sermons, ca. 1727–1772*. Colonial North American Project at Harvard. Andover-Harvard Theological Library, Harvard Divinity School.

Sylvanus Griswold Diary. East Lyme Historical Society.

Washington Papers. MountVernon.org and archive.gov.

Winthrop Papers. New London County Historical Society.

Bibliography

Periodicals

Connecticut Courant.

Connecticut Gazette.

The Magazine of American History 11 (1884); 13 (1885). New York: Historical Publication Company.

Norwich Packet.

Books

Bailyn, Bernard. *The Ideological Origins of the American Revolution.* Cambridge, MA: Belknap Press of Harvard University Press, 1992.

Bulkley, John. *An Impartial Account of a Late Debate at Lyme in the Colony of Connecticut.* New London, CT: Timothy Green, 1729.

Burr, Jean Chandler, ed. *Lyme Records, 1667–1730: A Literal Transcription of the Minutes of the Town Meetings with Marginal Notations, to which Hath Been Appended Land Grants and Ear Marks.* Stonington, CT: Pequot Press, 1968.

Burrows, Edwin G. *Forgotton Patriots: The Untold Story of American Prisoners during the Revolutionary War.* New York: Basic Books, 2008.

Bushman, Richard L. *From Puritan to Yankee: Character and the Social Order in Connecticut, 1690–1765.* Cambridge, MA: Harvard University Press, 1967.

Carrington, Henry B. *Battles of the American Revolution, 1775–1781.* New York: Promontory Press, 1974.

Caulfield, Ernest. *Notes on the History of Lyme and Old Lyme.* Lyme, CT: Lyme Historical Society/ Florence Griswold Museum, n.d.

Connecticut Military Record 1775–1848. Hartford: Connecticut General Assembly, 1889.

Cutler, Charles L. *Connecticut's Revolutionary Press*. Chester, CT: Pequot Press, 1975.

Deane, Silas. *The Deane Papers*. New York: New York Historical Society, 1887.

Finlay, Hugh. *Journal Kept by Hugh Finlay, Surveyor of the Post Roads on the Continent of North America 1773–1774*. Brooklyn, NY: Frank H. Norton, 1867.

Franklin, Benjamin. *Autobiography*. New York: Norton & Company, 1981.

Greenleaf, Jonathan. *Memoir of Reverend Jonathan Parsons*. Boston: American Quarterly Register, 1841.

Griswold, Wick. *Connecticut Pirates and Privateers*. Charleston, SC: The History Press, 2015.

Hale, Charles L., and Mary Babin. *Headstone Inscriptions: Town of Lyme, Connecticut*. Hartford: Connecticut State Library, 1937.

Hall, Charles S., ed. *Life and Letters of Samuel Holden Parsons*. Binghamton, NY: Otseningo Publishing Company, 1905.

Hoadly, Charles J. *The Public Records of the State of Connecticut*. Vols. 1 and 2. Hartford, CT: Case, Lockwood & Company, 1894.

Johnson, Reverend Stephen. *Election Sermon: Integrity and Piety the Best Principles of a Good Administration of Government*. New London, CT: Timothy Green, 1770.

Lehman, Eric D. *Homegrown Terror: Benedict Arnold and the Burning of New London*. Middletown, CT: Wesleyan University Press, 2015.

Loring, George B. *A Vindication of General Samuel Holden Parsons*. Salem, MA: Salem Press, 1888.

Maier, Pauline. *From Resistance to Revolution*. New York: Alfred A. Knopf, 1972.

Manstan, Roy R., and Frederic J. Frese. *Turtle: David Bushnell's Revolutionary Vessel*. Yardley, PA: Westholme Publishing, 2010.

Mather, Frederic Gregory. *The Refugees of 1776 from Long Island to Connecticut*. Albany, NY: J.B. Lyon Co., 1913.

Middlebrook, Louis F. *History of Maritime Connecticut during the American Revolution, 1775–1783*. Salem, MA: Essex Institute, 1925.

Perry, Charles E. *Founders and Leaders of Connecticut, 1633–1783*. Boston: D.C. Heath, 1934.

Peters, Reverend Samuel. *A History of the Reverend Hugh Peters*. New York: privately printed, 1807.

Pfeiffer, John. *Slavery in Southeastern Connecticut: A View from Lyme*. Old Lyme, CT: Old Lyme Historical Society, n.d.

Rogers, Ernest E. *Connecticut's Naval Office at New London During the War of the American Revolution*. New London, CT: New London County Historical Society, 1933.

———. *Sesquicentennial of the Battle of Groton Heights and the Burning of New London, Connecticut*. New London, CT: Fort Griswold & Groton Monument Commission, 1931.

Salisbury, Edward E., and Evelyn McCurdy Salisbury. *Family Histories and Genealogies*. N.p.: privately printed, 1892.

Searl, John. *A Funeral Sermon Delivered at Newburyport Dec 30, 1770 Occasioned by the Death of Mrs. Phoebe Parsons*. Boston: T&J Fleet, 1771.

Sill, Edward Everett. *A Forgotten Connecticut Patriot.* New Haven, CT: Tuttle, 1901.

Stark, Bruce P. *Lyme, Connecticut: From Founding to Independence*. Lyme, CT: privately printed, 1976.

Stiles, Ezra. *Extracts from the Itineraries and Other Miscellanies of Ezra Stiles, DD, LL.D, 1755–1794*. Edited by Franklin B. Dexter. New Haven, CT: Yale University Press, 1916.

———. *The Literary Diary of Ezra Stiles, President of Yale College.* Vols. 1, 2. Edited by Franklin B. Dexter. New York: Charles Scribner and Sons, 1901.

Storer, E.G. *Records of Freemasonry in the State of CT.* New Haven, CT: E.G. Storer Printer, 1859.

Trumbull, James Hammond, ed. *The Public Records of the Colony of Connecticut.* Hartford, CT: Brown and Parsons, 1850.

Trumbull, Jonathan, and Joseph Gurley Woodward. *Vindications of Patriots of the American Revolution.* Hartford: Connecticut Society of Sons of the American Revolution, 1896.

Truxes, Thomas M. *Defying Empire: Trading with the Enemy in Colonial New York.* New Haven, CT: Yale University Press, 2010.

———. *Irish-American Trade, 1660–1783.* Cambridge and New York: Cambridge University Press, 1988.

White, David O. *Connecticut's Black Soldiers, 1775–1783.* Chester, CT: Pequot Press, 1973.

Willauer, George J., Jr. *A Lyme Miscellany, 1776–1976.* Middletown, CT: Wesleyan University Press, 1977.

Woodward, Walter W. *Prospero's America: John Winthrop, Jr., Alchemy, and the Creation of New England Culture, 1606–1676.* Chapel Hill: University of North Carolina Press, 2013.

Zeichner, Oscar. *Connecticut's Years of Controversy, 1750–1776.* Chapel Hill: University of North Carolina Press, 1949.

Index

A

B

C

F

G

H

I

J

K

L

M

N

P

R

S

T

W

About the Authors

Jim Lampos and Michaelle Pearson live in Old Lyme, Connecticut. They have also authored *Remarkable Women of Old Lyme* (The History Press, 2015) and *Rum Runners, Governors, Beachcombers and Socialists* (Old Lyme Historical Society, 2010).

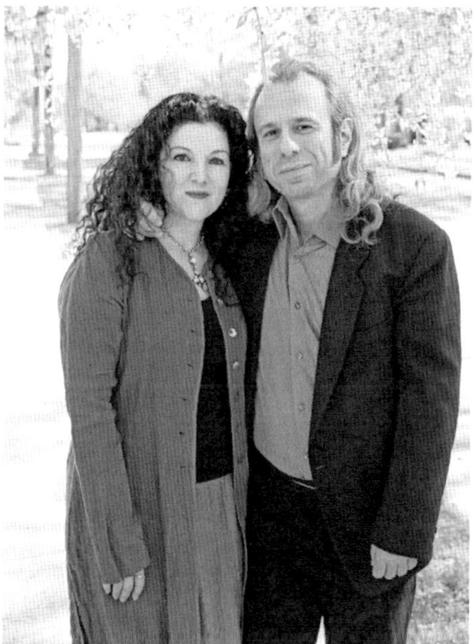

Jim Lampos and Michaelle Pearson on Lyme Street. *Courtesy of Angela Chicoski Photography.*